· AMERICA'S AGING ·

Productive Roles in an Older Society

Committee on an Aging Society
Institute of Medicine and National Research Council

NATIONAL ACADEMY PRESS
Washington, D.C. 1986

National Academy Press   •   2101 Constitution Ave., NW   •   Washington, DC 20418

NOTICE: The project that is the subject of this report was approved by the Governing Board of the National Research Council, whose members are drawn from the councils of the National Academy of Sciences, the National Academy of Engineering, and the Institute of Medicine. The members of the committee responsible for the report were chosen for their special competences and with regard for appropriate balance.

This report has been reviewed by a group other than the authors according to procedures approved by a Report Review Committee consisting of members of the National Academy of Sciences, the National Academy of Engineering, and the Institute of Medicine.

The Institute of Medicine was chartered in 1970 by the National Academy of Sciences to enlist distinguished members of the appropriate professions in the examination of policy matters pertaining to the health of the public. In this, the Institute acts under both the Academy's 1863 congressional charter responsibility to be an adviser to the federal government and its own initiative in identifying issues of medical care, research, and education.

This study has been supported by funds from the National Research Council Fund, a pool of private, discretionary, nonfederal funds that is used to support a program of Academy-initiated studies of national issues in which science and technology figure significantly. The NRC Fund consists of contributions from a consortium of private foundations including the Carnegie Corporation of New York, the Charles E. Culpeper Foundation, the William and Flora Hewlett Foundation, the John D. and Catherine T. MacArthur Foundation, the Andrew W. Mellon Foundation, the Rockefeller Foundation, and the Alfred P. Sloan Foundation; the Academy Industry Program, which seeks annual contributions from companies that are concerned with the health of U.S. science and technology and with public policy issues with technological content; and the National Academy of Sciences and the National Academy of Engineering endowments. The study was also supported by the Charles A. Dana Foundation.

Library of Congress Cataloging in Publication Data

Committee on an Aging Society (U.S.)
  Productive roles in an older society.

  (America's aging)
  "This report . . . presents the papers commissioned for a symposium on productive roles in an aging society"—Pref.
  Includes bibliographies and index.
  1. Aged—United States—Congresses. 2. Voluntarism—United States—Congresses. I. Title. II. Series. [DNLM: 1. Aged—congresses. 2. Voluntary Workers—congresses. WT 30 C7345p]
  HQ1064.U5C535 1986   305.2′6   85-63125

ISBN 0-309-03637-2

COMMITTEE ON AN AGING SOCIETY

This list shows affiliations of members at the time of their service with the committee.

Study Staff

ENRIQUETA C. BOND, Study Director and Director, Division of
   Health Promotion and Disease Prevention
DAVID TILSON, Study Director until September 1983
LINDA DEPUGH, Administrative Secretary

Consultant

GERALD S. SCHATZ

Preface

Substantial increases in the number and proportion of older persons in the decades ahead portend significant changes in American society. Indeed, demographic projections of a population rapidly growing older have led some observers to characterize the United States as an "aging society."

The ways in which an aging society might be a different society, in other than demographic characteristics, are not entirely clear. But it is evident that the changing age distribution of the population will have major implications, at the very least, for the following:

- financing, development, organization, and use of health care systems;
- patterns of family life, social relations, cultural institutions, living arrangements, and physical environments;
- distribution of jobs among older and younger workers, as well as the earnings, status, and satisfaction that these jobs may provide, within the context of age discrimination laws, seniority practices, and technological innovation;
- economic aspects of providing retirement income through various public and private mechanisms;
- quality of life of the population throughout the life course including functional status, well-being, legal status, and personal autonomy; and
- an ever-shifting agenda of related public policy issues.

If we are to deal effectively with these issues, our current understanding of the specific implications—for older and younger persons, for age relations, and for the institutions of our society—must be expanded.

The Committee on an Aging Society was organized to identify selected issues that need to be confronted, both soon and over the longer term. Recognizing that many organizations and ad hoc groups have been addressing a range of issues associated with aging and with older persons as an age group, the committee has attempted to emphasize broader societal issues as well. From among those issues the Committee on an Aging Society suggests topics that warrant systematic investigations fostered by the National Research Council, the Institute of Medicine, and other organizations. It is the committee's belief that such investigations of these topics will provide a basis for action by policymakers in both the private and public sectors.

This volume is the second report in a series, called America's Aging, in which the committee calls attention to issues that emerged from symposia convened to explore selected topics. Other reports or proposed symposia focus on health in an aging society, the social and built environment, and legal and ethical issues.

This report summarizes the committee's recommendations and the discussions on which they were based and presents the papers commissioned for the May 1983 Symposium on Unpaid Productive Roles in an Aging Society. Because many other groups have addressed the labor force participation of older persons, the committee chose to focus on unpaid productive roles to which less attention has been given.

FREDERICK C. ROBBINS
President
Institute of Medicine

Contents

· AMERICA'S AGING ·

Productive Roles
in an Older Society

Summary

INTRODUCTION

Speculation about an aging population's impact on American society has given rise to the identification of a wide range of issues, some relating to the quality of life throughout a lengthening life course, others relating directly to policymaking in both the public and private sectors. In framing the questions, some observers express anxiety that the growing proportions of older persons may place heavy burdens upon society. Others focus attention on the contributions that might be made to American life by the unprecedented numbers of older persons who will have withdrawn from the labor force but who are still healthy, vigorous, and rich in experience and skills.

Both perspectives are based on major assumptions, some of them perhaps unwarranted, regarding the nature and extent of productive activities. Little research is available to support the claims of either group of observers. Most of the research literature on productivity flows from traditional economic analyses of market activity. Unpaid productive activities are usually excluded from such analyses. As a consequence, and with an eye to the sets of issues outlined later in this chapter, the Committee on an Aging Society of the Institute of Medicine and the National Research Council convened a symposium on May 11–12, 1983, to explore what is known about unpaid productive roles and what

1

implications there might be for the future. The major issues considered in this summary chapter are definitions of productivity and the needs and contributions of older people in relation to unpaid productive roles.

Definitions of Productivity

Studies of unpaid productive roles are likely to require new concepts and new definitions of productivity. It is unclear to what extent models based on paid work roles will be useful in pursuing questions such as these: What unpaid activities are to be defined as productive? What are the relative numbers and characteristics of persons who are actually or potentially productive? How is unpaid productivity to be encouraged in different subgroups of the population? To what extent is age a meaningful index of actual or potential productivity?

It is perhaps unwarranted to make comparisons, explicitly or implicitly, between the factors that influence paid work and those that affect unpaid work. For example, in considering how many persons are engaged in unpaid productive activities, there is presently no clear basis for categorization comparable to that used by economists in counting the numbers of people who are in or out of the paid labor force.

This example is worth elaboration, for it suggests some of the conceptual pitfalls and unstated assumptions that may hinder our understanding of unpaid productivity if we attempt to generalize from paid productivity. Observers who are concerned about the burdens posed by an aging society often focus on the economic implications of the so-called *dependency ratio*, which is conventionally expressed as the size of the retired population relative to the size of the working population. Projected increases in the dependency ratio, occurring as the proportion of older persons rises in the decades ahead, are figuring more and more in many discussions of public policy. The capacity of the American economy to sustain the present responsibilities both of government and the private sector in providing supports to older persons is viewed as problematic.

To use the conventional dependency ratio in framing such issues, however, has major shortcomings, even when limited to the area of paid work. Most of the flaws have already been identified in the scholarly literature that deals with goods and services produced in the market.

One general problem lies in using the number or proportion of workers as the single major factor in assessing the productive capacity of the society. Productive capacity depends upon a broader set of factors, including the accumulation and utilization of capital and the rate of technological innovation. In certain sectors of the economy, such as agriculture, productivity has increased even as the number of workers has decreased precipitously. To take account of a fuller range of macroeconomic variables, questions relating to productive capacity are better expressed in terms of productivity per worker than in terms of numbers of workers.

A more specific problem in this area is that discussions of the dependency ratio are often focused exclusively on older persons as "the dependent population." This may well be an artifact of the recent preoccupation with the capacity of the Old Age and Survivors Insurance (OASI) trust fund to pay benefits to current and future beneficiaries. Nonetheless, it is evident that the dependent population in the United States is far from fully described by the number or proportion of older retired persons. Children and unemployed adults of any age are also economically dependent. When the full range of such dependents is expressed in the numerator of the dependency ratio, the economic implications of population aging appear in a different light. Recent studies have indicated that if birth rates remain low, a decline in "youth dependency" during the next decades may well moderate or even outweigh the economic significance of projected increases in "elderly dependency."

Even when children are taken into account, the number and proportions of dependent nonworkers are frequently described by using age as the proxy for labor force status. It is common to consider all persons below age 18 and all persons above age 64 as dependent and to consider all persons aged 18 to 64 as workers. However, significant numbers of persons under 18 and over 64 are in the labor force. Not only do two-thirds of older workers begin drawing Social Security benefits before they reach 65, but fewer than three of every four men aged 55 to 64 are presently in the labor force. Consequently, critics have appropriately argued that dependency ratios should be stated on the basis of labor force participation rates rather than on the basis of age.

Still another criticism is the frequent failure to differentiate among the needs of different types of dependents in considering the economic implication of population aging; that is, the relative economic needs of children, older persons, and nonworking adults younger than 65. Although substantial consideration has been given to differences in the income needs of retired persons and working persons, little attention has been paid to differences in household composition and to other major sources of heterogeneity within these population groups. How do the economic needs of a child differ from those of a single retired person? What are the marginal costs of supporting a second or third child within the same household? How does an older person's living arrangements affect that person's economic needs?

These various flaws in analyses that have been based on the conventional dependency ratio are becoming the subject of a growing body of critical literature. They are mentioned here because they suggest analogous confusions that might arise in considering unpaid productive work. It would be premature, for instance, to conclude that the need for unpaid services will increase only, or even primarily, among older people; that the numbers alone are useful predictors; or, conversely, that older people will be the only major source of new unpaid productivity in the society at large. Yet for the present those few social observers who are beginning to give attention to the significance of unpaid productive roles are focusing that attention upon older persons.

Unpaid Productive Roles: Needs and Contributions of Older Persons

Just as population aging is often perceived as posing macroeconomic burdens on society, larger numbers and larger proportions of older persons are frequently seen as generating an exponential increase in the need for health and social services. Although declines in mortality rates have been notable in this century, it is not clear if they have been accompanied by equivalent declines in morbidity. Optimistic predictions of the compression of morbidity in old age appear to be somewhat problematic, at least for the decades immediately ahead.

A substantial body of research literature indicates that although persons in their 60s and 70s now tend to be much healthier in the aggregate than ever before, the age-specific prevalence of long-term chronic diseases and disabling conditions rises exponentially in persons who are in their late 70s and 80s. The number of Americans in their late 70s and 80s will increase substantially in the coming years. It is projected that as early as the year 2000 half the people in the 65-and-older age category in the United States will actually be 75 and older, about 15 percent will be 85 and older. An unintended consequence of added longevity has been an increased prevalence of long-term disabling conditions that may well require a far greater quantity and range of health and social services than has been needed in the past.

For more than two decades, older retired persons have been envisioned as a new source of unpaid social and health services personnel. Sociologists and social psychologists writing in the early 1960s noted that work is a prime factor in determining one's social status and self-esteem in American society. Building upon this observation, they pointed out a need to create "new social roles" for retired older persons to enable them to recapture the status and the sense of self-worth that they may have lost with their departure from paid work. In the last two decades a number of small public and private sector programs have created formal mechanisms through which older persons have volunteered as social and health services workers.

Today, in the contexts of rapid population aging and the continuing trend of retirement at earlier ages, renewed attention is being paid to the roles that older persons might undertake in formal and informal institutions and in patterns of social relations. Of particular interest to many observers is whether the vast reservoir of active, healthy, experienced, and educated retired persons present in an aging society can be more effectively tapped, on an unpaid basis, to meet projected increases in demands for social and health services.

Although this question is of considerable interest, little systematic knowledge has been developed that could help in assessing this potential and the circumstances for its realization. What differential capabilities and desires exist within the older population to undertake unpaid productive activities? What types of activities? How will older persons be motivated? What are the formal and informal mechanisms through which such activities might take place? What are the conditions in which various kinds of formal organizations can effectively utilize unpaid activities? If the unpaid productive activities of older persons increase substantially in volume and/or range, what impact will this have on the social institutions and patterns of social relations in American life?

The Symposium on Productive Roles

Both sets of issues outlined above—(1) definitions of productivity and (2) the needs and contributions of older people in relation to unpaid productive roles—appeared to merit further inquiry; thus the Committee on an Aging Society planned a two-day symposium to explore these topics. Four invited papers were prepared: (1) "The Economics of Volunteerism: A Review" by Carol Jusenius Romero; (2) "The Older Volunteer Resource" by Jarold A. Kieffer; (3) "Unpaid Productive Activity Over the Life Course" by James N. Morgan; and (4) "Sociodemographic Aspects of Future Unpaid Productive Roles" by George C. Myers, Kenneth G. Manton, and Helena Bacellar.

These papers, which follow this summary chapter, were not intended to provide complete coverage or syntheses of existing knowledge but instead to inform and stimulate the committee's discussion. With the papers as background, the committee explored the subjects with the authors and came to several conclusions regarding needs for research that might usefully inform policy discussions and planning in both the public and private sectors. The balance of this chapter summarizes the symposium discussions and presents the committee's conclusions.

UNPAID PRODUCTIVE ROLES

Voluntary assistance to others, whether through formal organizations or through informal arrangements, is an honored American tradition. Its forms are varied: volunteer work for churches, cooperatives, civic clubs, charities, immigrant societies, hospitals, schools, museums, Foster Grandparents, the Peace Corps. Equally important are such unpaid activities as the home production of goods and services; time invested in raising children or in the care of ill relatives, friends, or neighbors; mutual support groups; and self-care. Compensated usually by friendship, conscience, and personal sense of worth, voluntary service is productive and important to the life of any community.

The aging of the population, in combination with changes in the economy, in health and social services systems, and in educational and other social institutions, will alter the needs that have traditionally been met by unpaid services. The numbers, skills, and needs of unpaid workers themselves will be different.

The assumption, however, that the increasing numbers of older people in the society will automatically generate greater needs for voluntary services, together with a greater supply of volunteers to meet those needs, is probably an oversimplification. The view that social needs are best or most effectively met by voluntary services is not yet substantiated by evidence.

In different words, the importance of voluntary activity is unquestioned, but it has been little studied and as a result is little understood. The forms, contributions, rewards, social and psychological dynamics, and efficiency of voluntary services vary widely. There is little understanding of the broad range of unpaid productive roles, whether performed by younger or older persons and whether inside or outside formal voluntary organizations. Neither is it clear if and how changes in the ways that unpaid productivity is valued will occur in an aging society.

Some of the questions can be phrased in more specific terms: What are the various forms of unpaid productive roles? How do they affect the well-being of the persons who give and the persons who receive help? What is their impact on the economy as a whole and on the social life of the community as a whole? How do we value the time and effort spent in unpaid roles? What incentives and disincentives do potential volunteers face? Are special problems encountered by older volunteers? What kinds of community problems are best met by voluntary services?

The answers to such questions will be important in planning to meet the changing needs of an aging society. There is some research literature on voluntary organizations, voluntarism, and altruism, but little of it is future-oriented and very few studies relate to demographic change.

In combination with other types of studies, the economic analysis of voluntarism is important, but it poses complex problems. There are no good measures of time spent in voluntary activities overall. Available data bases and time-use studies offer some clues, but these studies are inadequate and are unrelated to each other.

The value of volunteered time and service is difficult to measure. Value sometimes can be determined by figuring how much the work currently done by volunteers in formal organizations would cost if it were paid for; but other unpaid activities are so diffuse they defy accounting. There are process benefits and outcome benefits for both workers and clients that are important in social and psychological terms, but these also are difficult to translate into the usual economic indices. Another complicating factor is that in formal organizations volunteers have often been relegated to tasks comparable to low-paying jobs, a situation that is particularly common in organizations that rely heavily on women volunteers.

As the labor market, the labor force, the volunteer market, and the volunteer force change, the rewards of voluntarism are increasingly hard to pinpoint. How do people value their paid and their unpaid productive activity? What are different people willing to forgo to sustain their volunteer work? What opportunity costs do they pay?

Morgan (in this volume) notes that "as a society we are at some kind of peak in terms of the aggregate amount of productive time available in relation to the population." But although data are gathered regularly on paid work, surveys related to unpaid work are sparse. The available data show income first and then education as leading predictors of volunteer activity, but the data refer only to participation in formal organizations. Morgan comments further:

It is not available time that seems to drive philanthropic activity but abilities and purposes. People with children get involved in activities . . . that are directed at the socialization of their offspring. Active visible people are urged to take leadership roles, and the more money they give, the more they are asked also to give time. . . . Tax laws would appear to encourage more time donations, in comparison to money donations, among low-income people who do not itemize and cannot therefore get income tax rebates on their charitable contributions of money. But they may also be spending more time earning a living or looking for more paid work. . . . [P]aid work and unpaid work do not appear to be interchangeable and . . . the reduction in paid work hours with age, even after retirement, does not appear to lead to any substantial increase in volunteer work. Perhaps incentives are more important than free time. [Morgan, in this volume]

Incentives to unpaid productive work can be positive (e.g., friendship, societal contribution, identification with the welfare of the sponsoring institution or the persons being served) or they can be negative (e.g., in instances where there is no other choice but to perform an unpleasant duty). There has been relatively little systematic research on the motivations of voluntarism, despite the important implications both for government and for private organizations. Carol J. Romero (in this volume) emphasizes that the reasons people participate in volunteer organizations determine in part the extent to which voluntarism might substitute for reduced government provision of social services. If volunteers are motivated by societal need, "then the government could reduce expenditures in many areas with the expectation that volunteers would offset this reduction, at least to some extent." However, if volunteers are motivated by some personal benefit, however intangible, then reduction in government expenditures would elicit voluntarism only in those areas in which potential volunteers perceive potential benefits. In this case, she said, the government would need to be selective in its actions lest all social services be eroded. The extent to which altruism is a primary motivation remains unclear.

Questions also remain about what kinds of needs volunteers can be expected to meet and how. Romero observes:

Major changes are occurring within the American economy, changes that require increased volunteer activity. . . . [I]ncreasing demands are being placed on the voluntary sector to meet both immediate and long-term social needs. Furthermore, the aging of the population will lead to an increasing need for health care and other voluntary services for the elderly. The ways in which volunteers and volunteer organizations can, and will, respond to these changes are not really known. For example, there is an expectation—or perhaps more accurately, a hope—that older, retired people will become a major source of volunteers. It may well be, however, that many individuals will not be eager to volunteer. They may prefer instead to relax and enjoy themselves after a lifetime of work. . . . [Romero, in this volume]

Current knowledge of unpaid productive roles is inadequate in several other respects. There is no taxonomy of productive roles, no systematic delineation of points to be considered if studies of these phenomena are to be related to other studies in response to the society's needs for information. Some of the elements of such a taxonomy are the diversity, extent, and contribution of unpaid productive activity; individual and group social and psychological dynamics and their effects; and how these changing factors relate to each other and to changing local and societal values, needs, and capacities.

As Romero points out, the supply, demand, and mechanisms for allocation of voluntary services have yet to be modeled conceptually and empirically. In short, emerging knowledge of the field does not yet provide a satisfactory basis for judging how voluntarism figures in addressing individual and societal needs in a nation whose population is aging rapidly.

CHARACTERISTICS OF OLDER AMERICANS

Over the coming decades, older Americans on the average probably will be healthier, and it is evident that they will be better educated than their predecessors of the mid-twentieth century. Various demographic projections are based on different time intervals, however, and the projection strategies vary. Moreover, specific needs are difficult to deduce from the aggregated data. Nevertheless, current studies suggest important points in considering the needs and productive roles of older men and women.

Myers et al. (in this volume) consider pertinent sociodemographic trends. Expectations are that the portion of the population aged 65 and older will grow at a modest rate through the end of this century; the rate will then accelerate between 2010 and 2025 as the baby-boom generation reaches age 65. By 2025 the aged portion of the population is projected to be nearly 20 percent of the total. Life expectancy is predicted to increase substantially.

The proportion of older women will increase, especially the proportion of very old women. Currently, the proportions of widowed, separated, and divorced increase in successive age groups beyond age 55, with more than 30 percent of men and 75 percent of women in the over-75 age group living without spouses. This general pattern is expected to continue, but by 1995 there is also expected to be a slight rise in the proportion who will still be living in husband-wife households.

Successive groups of persons who reach old age will differ, for birth cohorts born at successive periods in history move through the life cycle in different ways as conditions and expectations change. For instance, far more older Americans in future decades will have had at least a high school education, and many will have had college educations. Many will have had job retraining and various other forms of adult educations. Already, many more women reaching 65 have had substantial work experience outside the home.

Labor Force Participation and Economic Status

Labor force projections cited by Myers et al. (in this volume) suggest that the pool of women outside the labor force and under age 60 will decrease over the next 20 years. (This is a group on whom many volunteer organizations have depended.) Both women and men, black and white, who will be out of the labor force at older ages will be numerically and proportionately greater, even in the group aged 60 to 69. Labor force projections by the Bureau of Labor Statistics indicate that paid work among older persons is not likely to increase significantly, which, according to Myers et al., seems to "support . . . the idea that other unpaid activities can be an alternative condition for sizable numbers in the growing older population." These projections are based on current labor force participation rates applied to census projections, however, and they do not yield a sufficiently clear picture. In particular, they do not take into account possible changes in the financial needs of older people.

Social Security, veterans' benefits, and retirement ages are changing—both up and down as many Americans retire as early as age 55 while others postpone retirement until their 70s. Raising Social Security entitlement ages would have little immediate effect on the size of the potential pool of volunteers among older people, but ultimately it would cut into that pool, as Myers et al. report.

How the financial status of the nation's older people will change is not known. Older Americans today are substantial consumers; and on the average the coming generations of older people are expected to be better off than those of today. Private pensions are a big factor in this regard, as is the recent income tax exemption of profits from a one-time sale of a family home for persons over 55 and other aged-based tax benefits. Still, many older Americans, especially members of minority groups and very old women, will not have been direct beneficiaries of these developments.

The debt structure that Americans will carry into their retirement years has been given little systematic attention. The dramatic rise in the price of housing in the last 20 years is an important factor. The cost of private and public transportation is increasing. Many families now are borrowing heavily for their children's educations. As pointed out in James N. Morgan's paper (in this volume), averages are not to be trusted because inequality in income and wealth increases with age. "An average does not tell how many are below some threshhold," and "among younger people, those with low incomes or no assets are not likely to stay that way; the older people in those circumstances are likely to remain so." If the number of well-to-do older Americans is increasing and the proportion of indigent older Americans (especially among the younger old) is decreasing, the coming generations of elderly may nevertheless be far from rich and free-spending.

Educational Levels

Educational attainment, as Myers et al. (in this volume) note, is widely viewed as positively related to high formal participation in voluntary and service organizations and important in explaining differences in self-help and activity levels. Yet forecasting educational attainment is almost neglected in official population projections. Working with data regarding levels of formal schooling, these authors found that older persons at the turn of the century will have much higher levels of formal education. Sharply lower proportions of older persons will have left school at the elementary or even high school level than is true of older persons today. Myers et al. expect educational attainment on the average to level off after the year 2000. "To the extent that formal educational attainment is positively related to more productive roles, then the next few decades should witness a great improvement in this regard. Of course, . . . we should balance this against the likelihood of higher labor force participation rates, especially for better educated women, for cohorts up to the time they reach the older ages."

Household and Family

The projections of household and marital status of older Americans yield similarly mixed implications. Myers et al. (in this volume) report that trends in household patterns, particularly women living alone, suggest that the demand for services may well increase, especially at the oldest ages. Yet there may be proportionately and numerically more persons in intact marriages who will therefore be in positions to supply services to spouses.

Kinship relations are an important and complicated but by no means clearly understood factor in both the need for services and the availability of people to meet those needs. Morgan (in this volume) observes that at present relatively little money is given to relatives outside the home. Less than 3 percent of a sample of persons were providing any financial support for parents who were around retirement age. Nor is much time given regularly to such unpaid activity as caring for grandchildren. Of particular importance, Myers et al. report, is the increased likelihood that persons reaching the older ages will themselves have parents still living. The effects of this situation can include strengthened family ties and a reduced need for social services, or they can include increased personal strain, especially for women care-givers, and an increased need for formal social services. In general, one effect is likely to be the reduction of the pool of potential volunteers for service outside the family.

Myers et al. go on to say:

It is likely, then, that there will be an enlarged pool of family members for whom mutual aid may be necessary. In turn, younger family members (at ages 65 to 69) are also available who could provide assistance if someone was in need. The term "potential" must be emphasized, inasmuch as the family support system depends on many other factors as well. These figures suggest that mortality conditions play a somewhat greater role than fertility in the structure of family relations and touch upon a whole range of issues relating to living arrangements, migratory patterns, and mutual aid and assistance. [Myers et al., in this volume]

Morgan (in this volume) points out that accessibility is a major factor in the availability of emergency aid within the family. The geographic mobility of Americans generally and new migrations of older Americans specifically raise questions not only about proximity of family members for care-giving but also about possible geographical mismatch of supply and demand for services for older people. If income, as Morgan suggests, is a highly important predictor of volunteer service, and if a substantial portion of financially able older Americans move to a few cities of the Sun Belt or segregate themselves in relatively wealthy communities, the poorer elderly, who may need more voluntary services, will be left in communities where there are fewer potential volunteers and fewer potential local donors of money and goods. This is not to suggest that the Sun Belt does not have or will not have low-income elderly persons or that older people of higher income levels do not need the kinds of services furnished traditionally by volunteers. Wealthy or not, new communities, even for retirees, seem to give rise to new volunteer involvements.

Health

Health status is a crucial determinant of productive activity and of the need for services of the kind that have always depended on volunteers. Here, too, information is inadequate, and the available projections have mixed implications.

Although people are living longer and on the average their health is better, Morgan (in this volume) observes that with advanced old age the dramatic increase in disabilities raises questions about the productive potential of an older population. And, as Myers et al. (in this volume) say, how relationships of age, disease, disability, and mortality are changing is a question of critical importance in determining both the demand for various types of volunteer services among the elderly and the potential pool of elderly who are healthy and able to provide such services.

Data from the National Health Interview Survey show that most Americans are relatively healthy into their mid-70s; but at the same time, rates of functional disability (some temporary, some long-term) rise by age 65, with the rates rising sharply after the mid-70s. In a population in which longevity is increasing, this means both a larger number of relatively healthy older people and an increasing number of ill and disabled persons. These changes in longevity, disease, and disability within the older population suggest that with longer lifetimes there will be more chronic disease and functional disability, but not until later in life than is the pattern today. More of the nation's elderly (the younger old) will be more mobile than their predecessors; at the same time, there will be a large number of very old persons who are unable to get around easily. The population as a whole is likely to include more individuals with visual and hearing problems. Projecting the nature and prevalence of the disease and disability that will occur with age depends on assumptions about advances in knowledge and medical care, and it calls for a projective epidemiology that has barely begun.

Again, to quote Myers et al.:

The use of projections that interrelate various population health states . . . does not resolve all of the issues in assessing health, health service utilization, and the implications of health for the supply of and demand for volunteer services. However, it does provide information on the basic parameters of such behavior for the system. The fact that relatively little effort has been applied to resolving the nature of such associations on a population level—let alone forecasting such relations into the future—indicates some serious gaps in the information base needed to plan for the requirements of an aging U.S. population. [Myers et al., in this volume]

If present trends continue, the United States' new older population will contain two subpopulations: the younger old, most of them healthy, and the older old, many of whom will remain relatively healthy until very advanced old age but more of whom will be chronically ill or disabled. The implication is that needs for various services will increase. Many older Americans will be contributing to these services, but it is not clear that the needs of older Americans can be met for the most part from within the older population. The frail elderly person in need of social and health services often poses labor-intensive activities requiring physical and physiological strength. Even the well and still-vigorous elderly may find these needs larger than those they can cope with either physically or psychologically.

The symposium participants knew of no existing national agenda for research to help policymakers anticipate the changing needs and capacities of the country's elderly. But other groups are neglected as well. All of this says nothing about the changing needs and capacities of successive groups of younger persons. Nor is any mention made of the extent to which the time and effort of older people may be required to care for younger family members, for children being reared in one-parent families, or for special groups of children such as the developmentally disabled. Services that may be needed (and forthcoming) from older people are not likely to be limited to recipients who are old.

OLDER AMERICANS AS A SOCIETAL RESOURCE

The symposium participants recognized the importance of productive activity to the well-being of many older persons and of the society at large, but they adopted no advocacy position encouraging older Americans (any more than younger Americans) to engage in unpaid roles.

Whether and in what circumstances more older people can and will donate time and effort to serving others are important questions. Simple analysis of survey data suggests that voluntarism—when defined as activity in or for a formal volunteer organization—declines with age; but to what extent this is a cohort effect rather than an effect of aging is unclear. Multivariate analysis, furthermore, suggests that this type of voluntarism is not age related; that educational level and income level are the more significant variables. Morgan (in this volume) notes also that the amount of leisure time is not a major factor. It is oversimple, then, to presume that if only age constraints were removed, retirees would constitute a ready pool of manpower and womanpower. The circumstances attending retirement vary. For some people, incentives may be more important than free time.

Incentives and Disincentives

Romero, Morgan, and Myers et al. (in this volume) all suggest that substantial proportions of today's retirement population have never shown any inclination to do volunteer work, and Romero finds specifically that volunteers in their retirement years are likely to be individuals who were volunteers earlier. This scarcely settles the matter. As mentioned earlier, studies of this subject deal principally with volunteering in formal organizations. Symposium participants pointed to the substantial assistance provided by family members and the proliferation of self-help and support groups and other less formal forms of unpaid productive activity. Many older people take very valuable unpaid roles (in family and neighborhood, for example) that have not been studied, and many may believe they are doing important work but in ways that are not being measured.

Morgan looks from a broader perspective at incentives, disincentives, and barriers affecting older persons' nonpaid productive activity and reports the following:

Multiple incentives are better than solitary ones, . . . all the barriers and most of the disincentives [should] be removed. . . .
Ordinary paid work in the usual marketplace is the least promising activity to expect older people to expand. Care for themselves and others is probably the most likely. . . .

Money incentives may well be less important, and affective rewards more important among older people. Both, however, are required. . . .

There are serious difficulties with the notion of increasing the altruistic unpaid work of older people. If there is no reciprocity or return benefit, the burden is likely to be quite unequal because of the unequal capacities and preferences of older people. [Morgan, in this volume]

The equity questions cannot be ignored, Morgan cautions: "For all our concern with incentives, it is crucial to remember that most differences in productive activity are the involuntary result of life histories, health, and an individual's particular environment. Attempts to increase economic incentives can result in rewarding the fortunate and punishing the unfortunate." For example, "the usual tax-break methods of encouraging things are particularly likely to be inequitable among the elderly. . . ."

Barriers to Organizational Voluntarism

Jarold A. Kieffer (in this volume) cites a variety of impediments to organizational voluntarism on the part of older persons: bias against age, fear of displacement of paid workers, and competing opportunities for leisure time. The social and psychological dynamics are especially important. Although some of these factors operate also at younger ages, Kieffer contends:

. . . like older people who work for pay or seek paying jobs, older persons, . . . serving as volunteers or looking for such assignments face many of the same kinds of age discrimination and discouragement policies and practices. . . .

. . . older people themselves are divided on the subject of their volunteerism. . . . Some are dubious about . . . what they perceive to be the "second class" status they feel often attaches to volunteer work. . . .

After lifetimes of work and contending, some people do not wish to get involved in activities that might entangle them with other people's problems. (This response is . . . opposite to that of people who like to focus on other people's problems in order to cope with their own—for instance, inactivity, isolation, or loss of purpose.) In other cases, older people . . . are skeptical about the value of what they would be doing or . . . they no longer feel they could tolerate bureaucratic practices. They fear demeaning assignments that other older volunteers have told them they can expect to receive. Or they do not wish to be placed under professional (and especially younger) supervisors, individuals they judge to be lacking in understanding about life and survival.

[P]rofessional staff are being inserted between volunteer governing board members and volunteers who make up the rank and file workers of organizations. . . . [W]hen paid professional vacancies develop, the "inside" professionals tend to pick . . . other professionals . . . from among the inside volunteers who might aspire to a paid job. . . . [V]olunteers become out of touch, ill-informed . . . , and dissatisfied . . . , people who may be around but who are definitely in the way. [Kieffer, in this volume]

Nevertheless, large numbers of older people do volunteer for work in private and public agencies,* and Kieffer says many more might do so if ways were opened for their useful participation. Surveys in 1981 in the United States indicated that in the group aged 55 to 64, 6.7 million persons engaged in volunteer work and 3.9 million more were interested in volunteering; in the 65-and-older age group, 5.9 million were involved in volunteer activities and 2.55 million more were interested in doing so. "No ready basis exists for judging either the number of additional older volunteers needed or the number who actually would respond to an expanded call for their help on a voluntary basis" (Kieffer, in this volume). And, as Kieffer, says, many who might volunteer might need training.

Many have not been asked. Older persons have not always been addressed specifically or appropriately in the recruitment of volunteers. Volunteers "will want to be assured that their . . . work is valuable . . . and that they are not being exploited as someone's drudge" (Kieffer, in this volume).

The discussion among participants left no doubt that volunteer service by older people would increase with improved incentives and the reduction of barriers. Some of these factors are easy to recognize but difficult to remedy; they require changes in organizational management and behavior as well as in budgeting. They also may require changes in law. Restrictions on use of volunteers by government agencies need review, Kieffer says. The value and effective use of volunteers are not well understood. Specific attention to the needs and assignments of volunteers has been valuable, illustrating the importance of volunteer coordinators. But the range of incentives to volunteering has not been given much attention. Training itself can be an incentive; lack of

---

*Volunteer activity in informal settings is not being considered here. Mobilizing this kind of activity will be much more difficult to accomplish as so little information exists about the incentives and disincentives that drive such activity.

insurance can be a disincentive. And the lack of reimbursement for out-of-pocket expenses for transportation, food, and other incidental expenses deters many people of low income and some of middle income from volunteer service. These points suggest the need for an agenda of research on the changing relationships of organizations, agencies, and the volunteers on which they depend, and on the implications for financing volunteer services.

New Community Settings

Kieffer also sees a need for large-scale demonstrations of the capacities and performance of older workers, and Morgan argues similarly for an "assessment of the 'human capital' of skills and experience among the retired and those soon to be retired."

Morgan argues also for new self-help and mutual-help institutions and communities. He urges "field trials" in stimulating the formation of communities in which all the barriers to productive activity among the elderly are dealt with simultaneously, and in which older persons could develop their own physical, economic, and social arrangements, to encourage all kinds of productive activities and to allow maximum choice. This is an argument not for segregation of the aged but for development of settings in which those without the usual support networks might better control their own circumstances. His example relates to care of the sick and disabled:

. . . Currently, in about half the cases this care seems take place in extremely expensive hospitals and nursing homes where costs are often out of control. Or sometimes this work is performed by a spouse at considerable physical, emotional, and sometimes financial costs (since the insurance schemes do not cover most of it). Extended families only rarely can be expected to help because they tend to be scattered and have their own children to care for. Natural communities do not develop. Indeed, most older people see their network of social support withering as their friends die, and the isolation in single-family homes does not encourage the development of new social support networks. [Morgan, in this volume]

The idea, Morgan says, is to open alternatives and opportunities, creating communities that will help the elderly to meet some of their own needs and that will yield lessons for communities elsewhere. This requires innovation in financing, too:

... For some kinds of new living arrangements to facilitate efficient self- and mutual help among the aged, what appears to be needed are some small development funds to assist the first attempts and export the successful mechanism. . . . Another important method is the use of nonamortized loans; older people may not always need or want to be accumulating further equity in their last years. There is an important difference between a project that covers its own costs, including interest on loans, and one that is subsidized or one that mimics condominiums for the young intent on saving taxes while building equities. [Morgan, in this volume]

Such efforts at creating new communities should not be one-time demonstrations. They should provide opportunities to examine problems that arise, means of solution, how people participate, what response mechanisms work, and how participants change over time. These would be different from the studies of residential settings for the aged, in which the usual focus has been on architecture and health care.

Symposium participants also saw a need to study the ways in which older residents interact in different neighborhoods and communities. How efficient are in-town retirement buildings, retirement communities, age-mixed neighborhoods, or old-age homes as places in which to live, not merely places in which to reside? How do various residential circumstances reduce demand for outside assistance? How much do residents do for themselves? How do these communities and neighborhoods function from the perspective of economics? How do productive roles change? Such questions merit systematic study.

CONCLUSIONS AND RECOMMENDATIONS

The Committee on an Aging Society convened a symposium focused on unpaid productive roles because it regarded this subject as having an important bearing upon two major sets of issues concerning the implications of population aging. One set of issues bears on the economic implications of the changing size of dependent subpopulations in relation to the per capita productivity of the working population. The other set of issues concerns the potential capacity of retired older persons to be productive in meeting social and health service needs in an aging society. Both sets of issues have been framed in earlier investigations in the context of traditional economic analyses of market activity. But those analyses have not given major attention to unpaid production, the circumstances in which it is undertaken, and its impact. The symposium was not intended to be comprehensive. Rather, it served as an opportunity to explore what is known and what needs to be known about unpaid productive activities in confronting the implications of an aging society. On the basis of this exploration the committee was able to reach several conclusions.

On the one hand, it is evident that there is a rich variety of unpaid productive activities being undertaken in contemporary American society by people of all ages. In addition to housework and volunteer activities that take place within formally organized volunteer organizations, there appears to be a great number of informal self-help and mutual support groups, as well as care-giving and social support for dependent family members, friends, and neighbors.

On the other hand, systematic information about these activities is sparse. Little is known about the types of incentives and capabilities that lead different people to undertake various unpaid productive roles, the volume of such activity that is taking place, and the social and economic impact of these activities. In the absence of such information it is difficult to anticipate the extent, nature, and social effects of the unpaid productive roles that older persons might undertake in an aging society. In short, neither government agencies nor private organizations have adequate conceptualizations or adequate information on unpaid productive roles.

Accordingly, the committee recommends that the National Research Council and the Institute of Medicine and other organizations foster scientific research on two broad topics to provide an informed basis for action by policymakers.

First, it is apparent that traditional economic analyses of market-oriented productivity need to be reformulated to incorporate productive activities that take place outside the market. The potential economic significance of such activities and the importance of interpreting and measuring them were generally noted by the National Research Council's 1979 Panel to Review Productivity Statistics. Such a reformulation, accompanied by measures that allow for paid and unpaid activities to be discussed in comparable economic terms, is particularly needed. If the volume of nonmarket productivity is as economically significant as many observers suspect it is, then policy choices framed by the conventional use of dependency ratios—such as in the debates regarding the levels of OASI or Medicare benefits our society can afford—will be poorly informed.

Second, it appears that the demographic, psychological, social, and ethical dimensions of unpaid productive activities warrant systematic investigation. Who are the persons who undertake such activities? What are the incentives that motivate them? What is the nature and extent of such activities in a variety of informal and formal settings? What is the contemporary impact of unpaid productivity on social institutions and patterns of social relations? Are such impacts likely to become magnified in the context of population aging? Are the activities that older persons may wish to contribute likely to match the needs of society? And what are some of the ethical questions? Should older people be encouraged to do work no one is willing to pay for? Or to undertake, without payment, some of the jobs that people who need the money are now getting paid to do? A far better base of knowledge about unpaid productive roles is necessary if we are to anticipate the implications of such issues for an aging society.

BIBLIOGRAPHY

National Committee on Careers for Older Americans. 1979. *Older Americans: An Untapped Resource.* Washington, D.C.: Academy for Educational Development. Presentation of argument for increased and more flexible employment and voluntary opportunities for older persons.

National Institute on Aging. 1983. *Special Report on Aging 1983.* Publ. No. 83-2489. Bethesda, Md.: National Institutes of Health, August. Discussion of current demographic and health status research relating to productive roles of older persons.

Panel to Review Productivity Statistics, Committee on National Statistics, Assembly of Behavioral and Social Sciences, National Research Council. 1979. *Measurement and Interpretation of Productivity.* Washington, D.C.: National Academy of Sciences. Detailed examination of the inadequacy of conventional measures of productivity both for wage-price decisions and for broader economic assessments.

Schindler-Rainman, E., and R. Lippitt. 1975. *The Volunteer Community: Creative Use of Human Resources.* 2d ed. San Diego: University Associates. Discussion of and annotated bibliography on the organizational use of volunteers.

U.S. Department of Commerce, Bureau of the Census. 1983. *America in Transition: An Aging Society: 1982.* Current Population Reports, Special Studies, Series P-23, No. 128. Washington, D.C.: U.S. Government Printing Office. Recent projections of the age of the U.S. population.

The Economics of Volunteerism: A Review

Carol Jusenius Romero

The role of the volunteer in America has become a topic of public interest, mainly because of the confluence of three trends. First, all levels of government are encouraging volunteer work as a substitute for government's declining role in the provision of social services. Second, women—historically the source of much volunteerism in America—have been entering the work force in increasing numbers. Finally, growth in the size of the retired population has led to discussion of ways to use the time, talents, and energy of older people. But although there is interest in understanding and encouraging volunteerism, relatively little is known about the activity.

Volunteerism is often perceived as donations of time or labor but it can also include donations of money or goods, and in each of these forms it varies widely along several dimensions.

Volunteer activities take place in settings that have different degrees of structure and formality. Such activities may be quite informal, occurring in a casual, unstructured way; or they may be organized but not performed within a formally structured group; or both the activity and the group may be structured and formally organized. To illustrate: volunteer activities range from a neighbor helping a neighbor, to a group of parents organizing to

Carol Jusenius Romero is staff economist at the National Commission for Employment Policy, Washington, D.C.

clean a playground, to a formal volunteer group, such as the PTA or Volunteers of America, performing formally specified functions.

Volunteer activities also vary in their time requirements. People may participate in them from 1 to 52 weeks in a year, any day of the week, and for any number of hours. Some activities are spread out over weeks or years; others are concentrated (for example, within communities after a disaster strikes).

Finally, volunteering, like other activities, usually has some unpleasant aspects, and for people to be willing to undertake unpleasant tasks they must be compensated in some fashion. Compensation for volunteering can take a variety of forms. Sometimes a volunteer receives only psychic, personal satisfaction, or there may be some public recognition. A range of monetary compensations exists as well. Some people receive income tax deductions for their donations. There are also more direct means of monetary compensation. For example, the Foster Grandparent program gives participants a stipend to supplement their income, and people who work for the Salvation Army earn their entire income from this activity. To the extent that the earnings of these individuals are less than could be obtained in another type of work, this differential is equivalent to donating money or time.

A key question of this paper is why people volunteer. Is altruism the primary motivation, or do people volunteer out of some form of self-interest? Are people motivated "to volunteer" in general, or are they motivated to volunteer for particular types of activities? Such questions highlight an important policy area. If volunteerism is to be promoted to meet social needs, then the mechanisms that encourage volunteerism must be understood.

Survey results suggest a range of reasons for volunteering. According to the data in Table 1, nearly 30 percent of people who volunteer time "thought [they] would enjoy doing the work; feel needed." Almost 25 percent volunteered because a child, relative, or friend was involved, and 11 percent reported that they wanted work experience. Generally, motivating forces include children, relatives, and friends; religious beliefs; political or social concerns; personal history or interest in the activity; social pressures; and a desire to keep busy, feel productive, meet new people, or interact socially.

The large percentage of multiple responses shown in the table

TABLE 1   Reasons for First Becoming Involved in a Volunteer
Activity

Reasons	Percent of Adult Volunteers
Wanted to do something useful; help others; do goood deeds for others	45
Had an interest in the activity or work	35
Thought I would enjoy doing the work; feel needed	29
Had a child, relative, or friend who was involved in the activity or would benefit from it	23
Religious concerns	21
Wanted to learn and get experience; work experience; help get a job	11
Had a lot of free time	6
Thought my volunteer work would help keep taxes or other costs down	5
Other	1
Don't recall	5
Total	181[a]

[a]Total exceeds 100 percent because of multiple responses.

SOURCE: Gallup Organization, Inc., *Americans Volunteer.* Survey for Independent Sector (Princeton, N.J., June 1981).

suggests that individuals volunteer for a combination of reasons: No one motive, taken alone, is likely to be sufficient. After all, not every parent volunteers for a child-related activity and not every religious person volunteers for a church–synagogue or social welfare cause.

This paper stems from my work dealing with people's willingness to volunteer for formal organizations. The data and research cited here reflect that focus, although as indicated later many of the issues are applicable to other forms of volunteering as well. The paper is divided into four sections. The first presents data on Americans' unpaid work for formal volunteer organizations; it provides a backdrop to the analyses that follow. The next section reviews a number of economic analyses of this type of volunteering to determine how the motivation to volunteer has been analyzed conceptually and empirically and why motivations matter for public policy. The third section suggests areas for future research on volunteerism, and the final section gives a brief summary and offers some concluding thoughts.

WORK WITHOUT PAY FOR FORMAL ORGANIZATIONS

About 75 percent of the work people do without pay is for formal organizations.[1] The amount of time people spend in this way and the types of organizations for which they volunteer are discussed below.

Amount of Time

The proportion of Americans who volunteer has risen somewhat over the past 20 years. In 1965, 21 percent of women and 15 percent of men did some volunteer work. By 1981, participation in volunteer activities had risen to 28 percent among women and 30 percent among men.[2]

Although these figures may suggest a fairly widespread involvement in volunteer activities among Americans, a few cautions are in order. First, the proportions are small compared to the percentages of men and women who are either working or looking for work (77 percent of men and 53 percent of women are currently in the work force). Second, few people volunteer on a continual basis. While cross-sectional data indicate that about 25 percent of middle-aged women volunteer in a given year, longitudinal data reveal that fewer than 15 percent volunteer year after year.[3] Looking at it another way, fewer than 50 percent of women volunteers in one year had volunteered more than once in the recent past.

Other data on middle-aged women who volunteer illustrate some of the range of variability in the amount of time spent volunteering. Of all women who volunteer, the average participation time is 24 weeks per year; approximately 25 percent of those women, however, spend between 49 and 52 weeks in this activity. The average volunteer time per week for middle-aged women is 6 hours. More than 60 percent of women spend between 2 and 7 hours, 10 percent spend 1 hour, and another 10 percent spend 15 or more hours.[3]

Data on men close to or at retirement age reveal similar variations in the amount of time spent volunteering.[4] The 20 percent who volunteer spend, on the average, 24 weeks per year in the activity. About one-third of the volunteers participate 49 to 52 weeks and another one-third participate for 4 or fewer weeks. During the weeks of volunteering the men average 7 hours in this activity. More than 60 percent of the men spend between 2 and 7 hours, about 10 percent spend 1 hour, and more than 10 percent spend 15 or more hours.

Types of Volunteer Activities

There are many different types of formal organizations for which people volunteer. Unfortunately, however, the available data do not permit distinguishing among organizations according to measures of either their social usefulness or the extent to which volunteers must engage in unpleasant tasks to carry out the organizations' goals. Still, these data do illustrate the broad range of volunteer activities and the fact that different activities seem to appeal to different types of people.

Formal volunteer activities range from the PTA to soup kitchens to political and social causes. For instance, in 1981, 10 percent of the adult population volunteered for religious activities, 12 percent volunteered at hospitals or in other health-related activities, another 12 percent volunteered for school-related activities, 1 percent worked as poll watchers, 4 percent worked as campaign workers—the list goes on.[5]

It appears that sex and age play a role in the types of organizations for which people volunteer.[6] Men are more likely than women to participate in recreational and work-related activities; women are more likely to participate in health, educational, and religious activities. Further, adults are more likely than teenagers to volunteer for political and work-related activities, while teenagers are more likely to volunteer for health, recreational and educational activities.

Longitudinal data confirm that as people age, they change the type of organization for which they volunteer.[7] Among women 37 to 51 years of age, 28 percent of the volunteers participated in school activities and in such groups as Boy Scouts or Girl Scouts; 33 percent did church-related work; and another 30 percent volunteered for hospitals, clinics, major community drives, and other social welfare or civic causes. Five years later, the women volunteers (aged 42 to 56) had somewhat shifted their patterns of volunteering. Fewer volunteered for schools and other child-related activities (less than 20 percent), and more volunteered for both church-related activities (over 40 percent) and for hospitals, clinics, community drives, and civic causes (over 30 percent).

Taken together, these data suggest a richness and complexity in the amount and type of unpaid work that occurs in this society. The next section reviews analyses of the motivations that underlie the decision to volunteer.

ECONOMIC ANALYSES OF THE REASONS FOR VOLUNTEERING

The economist's approach to analyzing the motivation to volunteer is twofold: first, develop a behavioral model, and, second, derive hypotheses from the model and test them empirically. The empirical tests—typically some form of regression analysis—seek to disentangle the various determinants of people's actions. For example, a text might ask how parents' participation in volunteer activities is influenced by the presence of children in the family, while simultaneously taking into account the parents' educational levels, incomes, and work patterns.

The research reviewed here has been selected to illustrate the economist's approach to the issue of why people volunteer. And as such, these illustrations admittedly are not without limitations. Nevertheless, they can be used to stimulate thought and discussion about areas of study and suggest directions for future research.

In the studies described below, two types of reasons for volunteering are considered: (1) satisfaction derived from helping others and (2) direct personal benefit, independent of the extent to which others are helped. These research efforts examine whether altruism or personal benefits alone underlie an individual's motivation to volunteer, how family considerations influence a person's volunteerism, and the reasons why motivations of volunteerism are important to public policy.

Volunteering Motivated by Altruism

One of the first modern-day economic discussions of volunteerism is found in an article by Kenneth Boulding.[8] Boulding suggested that although philanthropy—or volunteerism—is often viewed as a transfer payment, for which there is no obvious reciprocation, from one individual to another, it may be more useful to look at the benefits received by the giver for being philanthropic. Boulding proposed two ways in which the giver may be compensated: (1) "a certain glow of emotional virtue" for having been philanthropic and (2) recognition that there is a "common identity in humanity."[9]

These two ways would now be called "altruism" by economists.[10] The reward for volunteering motivated by altruism is simply a good feeling for having been helpful to others. However, more direct rewards for volunteering also exist (as indicated earlier by the data in Table 1 on the reasons people say they volunteered). Some of the research efforts involving more direct rewards for volunteerism are discussed below.

Experience As Compensation for Volunteering

Two studies[11] tested the hypothesis that volunteerism is a form of personal investment; that is, people volunteer to enhance their future job and income prospects. Under this view, the fact that volunteerism benefits others is coincidental; it is not an important motivation.

The first article argues that women volunteer as a way of preparing for (re)entry into the job market—to gain experience and information about possible future jobs.[12] This hypothesis was tested on a sample of women who had been in graduate school between 1945 and 1951 using two dependent variables: hours of volunteering in a year and hours of volunteering for organizations other than professional societies.

Two of the study's independent variables were intended to represent "a desire for training" in preparation for (re)entry into the work force: (1) whether or not the woman was planning to work in the near future and (2) the average comparable market wage of the volunteer work that was done (a measure of the skill content of the activity). The results of the study showed that both variables were positively related to volunteerism and statistically significant.[13]

The author interpreted her results as follows:

Women, at least those in the education, income and age group most actively participating in volunteer work, appear to be doing so in part for their own families but also to a great extent for themselves—to build and maintain their human capital to aid in the job search.

... the volunteer organization remains one of the few institutions accessible to these women for the important activity of maintaining or building human capital.[14]

The results seem plausible for women of this particular age and educational level. At the same time, however, there are some limitations to the empirical work that call the results into question.

First, the variable "comparable market wage of volunteer work" need not be interpreted as an indicator of a desire for training, but instead may indicate the status content and desirability of different types of volunteer work. Women volunteering for desirable, high-status activities may spend more hours volunteering than women who are in less desirable, lower-status organizations or positions.

Second, the test of the variable "plans to work in the future" is not "clean." This variable has been constructed in such a way that women who are out of the labor force and plan to look for work are compared to two groups combined: those who do not plan to work and those who are already working. A "cleaner" test of the hypothesis would have been to include only the former—those not employed and not planning to look for work—in the reference group.

The inclusion of women who are already employed confuses the issue. Because they are employed, they may supply fewer hours of volunteer labor, but the reason for this reduction is not clear: either they may not desire to (re)build their skills or they simply may have less time to volunteer. There is also no information about the relative number of employed and unemployed women. Because of these limitations, it is impossible to state with certainty that volunteerism is used by women as a vehicle for easing (re)entry into the job market.

In the second article, Menchik and Weisbrod tested volunteerism as a form of investment by positing that people may volunteer because it "raises one's future income by providing work experience and potentially valuable contacts."[15] An alternative hypothesis was also posed: People may consider volunteer time to be a type of consumer good, something to be enjoyed or consumed. In contrast to the investment hypothesis, the consumption hypothesis posits that people volunteer because they enjoy either the activity or the product of the activity. Under this view, there are no negative aspects to volunteering for which compensation is necessary.

These hypotheses were tested with a sample of working people drawn from a national survey. Nearly two-thirds of those surveyed were married men with a wife at home full-time; the remainder were single heads of households, many of whom were likely to be women. To allow for possible differences among types of volunteer activities, there were several dependent variables, all assessed in terms of hours: (1) total volunteer work, (2) volunteer work for elementary and secondary education, (3) volunteer work for higher education, (4) volunteer work for welfare, and (5) volunteer work for natural resources (environment).

The competing hypotheses were tested empirically by including a person's wages as an independent variable in the regression. Wages measure the opportunity cost of volunteering; that is, the money forgone by spending time not working for pay. If people view volunteerism as a form of consumption, an inverse relationship between wages and volunteering would be expected. People make trade-offs between working (earning wages) and volunteering; the higher the wage rate, the less likely a person is to spend time volunteering rather than working. By contrast, if people view volunteerism as a form of investment, a positive relationship between wages and volunteerism would be expected. The reasoning is as follows: "If those with greater ability to benefit from volunteer work also earn more per hour in the absence of volunteer work, we have a situation in which higher wage workers may volunteer more hours than lower wage workers...."[16]

The results of the study indicated that the relationship between wages and hours of volunteerism is positive, which is consistent with the hypothesis that volunteerism is a form of investment. However, this interpretation of the results is questionable, because there are problems with the underlying theory. First, rather than expecting a positive relationship between wages and volunteerism under the investment hypothesis, it would seem more reasonable to expect an inverse relationship. People with low wages might have a greater desire to enhance their future earnings than people with high wages. To the extent that volunteering is a way of increasing future earnings, low-wage earners could be expected to volunteer more (not less) than high-wage earners.

A second problem concerns the empirical test of the alternative hypotheses. Using a wage variable assumes that the only way working people spend time volunteering is by giving up time for paid employment. However, casual observation suggests that people also volunteer after work, in the evenings, or on weekends. In other words, time for volunteering can also come from time that would otherwise be devoted to either housework or leisure.

The Effect of Family Obligations on Volunteering

This author's research raised more general questions about the factors influencing volunteerism. One concern was to determine the circumstances under which a person would volunteer, notwithstanding household obligations.[17] Specific research questions focused on the relationship between volunteerism and the movement of older Americans into retirement.

The research built on previous work analyzing how individuals, operating within a family setting, make decisions about spending their time (or money).[18] Each family member divides his or her time among three major categories: (1) work outside the home, (2) work inside the home, and (3) leisure. The precise way time is allocated to these categories mirrors the entire family's preferences for goods bought in the market, goods produced at home, and leisure. By selecting the combination that maximizes its utility (or happiness), the family simultaneously allocates its members' time.

Maximizing household utility may require that a husband and wife use their time differently over the family's life cycle, particularly with regard to their division of market and nonmarket (or home) work and depending upon their comparative advantages in these two activities. For example, over its life cycle a family will generally be willing to have the woman spend proportionately more time working full- or part-time at home, since men are typically more productive—in the sense of earning more—in the job market than in home work.

Including volunteerism as a way people may spend their time required the addition of detail to this model. The first argument to be considered was that people must be compensated for volunteering. Such compensation may be:

- direct increased personal satisfaction due to "a feeling of virtue," meeting new people, interacting socially, feeling productive, or keeping busy;
- increased welfare of another family member (This case recognized that a person operates within a family and that the output from one person's work increases the goods and services that another family member may enjoy.), and
- increased welfare of people outside the family. (Of the three motivations for volunteering, this is the least tangible and represents the closest approximation to altruism.)

Second, it was posited that not all household decisions regarding the use of time (or money) are equally important. Those involving smaller portions of a household's time (or money) are usually less important than those involving larger portions and are made independently of major household decisions. (For example, a decision to buy shoes or a tablecloth will be made independently of a decision to buy or rent a house.)

Decisions about the amount and timing of work outside and inside the home (including child care) are of major importance to a family. Entering the job market—or raising children—typically requires a substantial time commitment on the part of household members. Also, the lack of flexibility usually found in the number and timing of hours of paid employment and the continual nature of child care make these decisions more complex.

By contrast, the decision to volunteer may be either of major or minor importance to a family. It need not consume a sizable portion of a household's time (or income), and the amount and timing of volunteerism is generally flexible.

Volunteerism, then, was hypothesized to assume a smaller role in a family's life when the benefits accrue only to people outside the family. Families would be unlikely to reduce their income, their home-produced goods, or their leisure by sizable amounts in order to help people not in the household. Only after the demands of household members have been satisfied would families volunteer in this way.

However, if a family member (such as a child) benefits from the volunteering, it was hypothesized that volunteerism would assume greater importance and in fact would become a form of homework. In this case, a family may be willing to (1) alter its original combination of market- and home-produced goods and leisure and (2) consume either fewer market goods or less leisure in order to have more home-produced goods.

This view of volunteerism suggested some specific questions concerning the reasons why people volunteer:

• In which situations are people willing to give up work time to volunteer?

• Are people more likely to volunteer when a family member (including the volunteer) receives some of the benefits from that volunteerism?

• Are people who live in areas with concentrations of people outside the family who need assistance (such as in cities) more likely to volunteer than those who live outside such areas?

Regarding retirement issues specifically:

• Are retired people who have leisure time more likely to volunteer than those who are fully employed? (Economists would argue that because the opportunity cost of their time is smaller than among those who are employed, they would be more likely to volunteer.)

• Are people who have an independent source of income sufficient to meet household obligations—such as retired people with sizable pensions and savings—more likely to spend time volunteering than those whose major source of income comes from their current job?

The data used to address these questions were collected in the National Longitudinal Surveys of older men and older women.[19] For the men, there was one dependent variable: whether or not they volunteered in 1978. The women's data permitted differentiating among types of volunteer activities. Four dependent variables were used: whether or not the women volunteered (1) generally, (2) for a church activity, (3) for a child-related activity, and (4) for a social welfare or civic activity.[20]

General results for the men indicated that volunteerism is greater among the more educated and among those who live outside urban areas and in places with low unemployment rates; older men do not appear to volunteer more in areas with greater social needs. Also, at this stage of their lives (when they are in their late 50s to early 70s), men are not influenced to volunteer by the presence of children in the family, possibly because the children are usually older.

General results for the women indicated that volunteerism is greater among the more educated and among those with a history of volunteering, but it does not differ between urban and nonurban areas or between areas of high and low unemployment. The influence of children on women's volunteering differs by the type of volunteering that is done. Children raise the probability that a woman will participate in child-related activities, but children do not affect the probability that a woman will volunteer for other types of activities.

The detailed investigations of volunteerism among women indicated that it is important to distinguish among types of volunteer work. The relationship between volunteerism and several of the independent variables (that is, in addition to the children variable already mentioned) differed by the type of activity. Of special importance, given the questions raised earlier, was the result that the effect of employment varies by type of activity. Women who volunteer for child-related activities are likely to give up work time to do so. Women who volunteer for church-related activities tend to work fewer hours during the week, but they do not necessarily work fewer weeks in a year. Finally, the amount of time women work throughout the year and during any given week does not appear to influence their participation in social welfare or civic activities.

Specific results on the retirement issues indicated that policies affecting the amount of time people work are likely to have different effects on the participation of men and women in volunteer activities. Men are unlikely to be affected; their volunteerism was not found to depend upon their current employment or retirement status. Policies that permit moving from full- to part-time work, however, may increase women's participation in church-related activities.

Other results on the retirement issues indicated that policies concerning the amount of income people have during retirement may affect men and women in different ways. Older men with lower levels of income from assets volunteer less. Older women with lower levels of such income are less likely to volunteer for social welfare causes; however, income was not found to be related to women's participation in either church- or child-related activities.

These results raise several questions. For example, distinguishing among types of volunteer activities is important for
studies of women volunteers; it is therefore plausible that such
distinctions are equally important for men. Also, it would be
useful to explore why several factors seem to have different
effects on the participation of women in the various volunteer
activities. For instance, is volunteer time more flexible in social
welfare activities so that people do not need to trade off paid
employment to participate? Alternatively, does volunteering for
church-related efforts carry with it a special form of gratification? Are people willing to make some trade-offs with paid
employment to gain this kind of gratification, whereas they
would be unwilling to make the same trade-offs for social welfare
activities?

Policy Implications of the Reasons for Volunteering

The question of whether people volunteer to gain some benefit
for themselves or to help others outside the family carries with it
certain policy implications. The reasons why people volunteer
determine in part the extent to which volunteerism could substitute for reduced government provision of social services. If people
volunteer because of social needs, then governments could reduce
expenditures in many areas with the expectation that volunteers
would offset this reduction, at least to some extent. However, if
people volunteer for some personal benefit, then a reduction in
government expenditures would elicit more volunteerism only in
those areas that offer the greatest benefits to the volunteers. In
this case, governments would need to be selective in their actions
if adequate levels of all social services were to be maintained.

Menchik and Weisbrod tested this issue empirically through
the question: Do government expenditures "crowd out" volunteerism?[21] (Crowding out implies that there is a finite amount of
"need" and that government involvement effectively substitutes
for involvement on the part of private citizens.) The authors
argued that if individuals volunteer because they expect to
derive personal benefits in the future as a result of the activity
(the investment hypothesis given earlier), then government
involvement has no predictable effect on volunteerism. However,
if volunteerism is undertaken for its own sake (the consumption
hypothesis), then governments could conceivably crowd out pri-

vate sector volunteerism. Under the consumption hypothesis, individuals would be less likely to volunteer for a cause if at least some of the needs of that cause were being met by government expenditures. To test for the possibility of government crowding out volunteerism, Menchik and Weisbrod included an independent variable in the regression: per capita state and local government expenditures in different program areas in the state where the individual lived.

The results on the crowding out issue were mixed. In the areas of elementary and secondary education and natural resources, greater government expenditures were associated with fewer hours of volunteering. But there was no significant relationship between government expenditures and volunteering in the areas of higher education and welfare. The inconclusive nature of the test results led the authors to suggest that the crowding-out issue merits further study.

It should be noted, however, that there is a limitation to the theoretical approach that was taken in this study. Under the consumption hypothesis, people may volunteer either because they enjoy the process—the activity itself—or because they enjoy the product of that activity. (For example, people may volunteer to clean a park because they enjoy being out-of-doors or because they enjoy a clean park.) Even under the consumption hypothesis, the extent to which government involvement could crowd out volunteerism might differ depending upon why people volunteer. (If the park is already clean and people enjoy being outside, they may find other ways to both volunteer and be out-of-doors simultaneously.) The test of the crowding-out issue considered the case in which people volunteer to gain the product; it did not consider that people may enjoy the activity itself.

The results of the empirical test on crowding out are puzzling. No explanation was given as to why crowding out might occur in some program areas but not in others. Also, the authors did not explain how crowding out occurs given that (1) crowding out is only possible under the consumption hypothesis, and (2) their earlier results indicated that volunteerism is a form of investment, not consumption.

This seemingly contradictory result may be explainable. Menchik and Weisbrod neglected to consider that crowding out could occur even if people view volunteerism as a form of investment. Government involvement would presumably reduce the probability that either volunteer organizations would exist or that they would require large numbers of volunteers. And it is these organizations and these volunteer positions that provide the institutional setting for volunteerism.

In sum, the specifics of this approach are not particularly satisfying, but the question the authors have posed remains important. Do government expenditures substitute for volunteerism and will a reduction of government involvement in social welfare and other areas call forth more volunteerism?

Lessons From Past Research

It is apparent from this review that economists do not agree on the motivations for volunteering. On some points their results are inconclusive. For example, while some studies may find that volunteerism is a form of investment, there are a sufficient number of questions about the research to cast doubt on the findings. On other points, such as the trade-off between work time and volunteering among women, the evidence is insufficient to state findings with certainty. Like most research questions, the issue needs to be investigated with more than one approach and one data set before it can be considered to be resolved.

On two points, however, the research is consistent. First, participation in formal volunteer organizations is largely a middle- and upper-class phenomenon. Most people who volunteer in this way have higher levels of education and income than those who do not. Second, an underlying view presented in the articles is that people must be compensated personally for volunteering.[22] Altruism is unlikely to be a sufficient motivation, and it is not reasonable to expect people with more leisure time, such as those who are retired, necessarily to be interested in using their free time to volunteer.

WHERE DO WE GO FROM HERE?

This section suggests three categories of research in the area of volunteerism. Two focus on the individual volunteers: descriptive data on the nature and extent of people's participation in volunteer activities and analyses of their motivations to volunteer. The third category concerns volunteer organizations and includes analyses of the role of the "voluntary sector" in the total economy.

Data on Volunteerism

At the outset of this paper, there was a description of the three ways people volunteer—donations of time, money, and goods— and of the range of variability possible in carrying out these activities (i.e., volunteerism occurs in settings that have different levels of organization and structure, its timing is often flexible, and there are different ways that people are remunerated).

Several data sources give an empirical content to this picture: for example, the 1973 Survey of Giving, the 1981 Gallup survey, and the National Longitudinal Surveys. These data bases and their findings, however, are not always readily available to researchers, policymakers, or program operators. The findings of these sources could be summarized to provide a useful inventory of volunteerism. This inventory could include documentation of the range of variability in the amount and types of volunteerism, analyses of the reasons for different findings among data bases, and a resulting rough set of summary statistics on volunteerism. To provide a complete picture some new data may also be required.

The purposes of this work are twofold: (1) to suggest both the areas in which volunteerism could potentially substitute for government expenditures and the groups of people who would most likely respond to an increased need for volunteers; and (2) to assist more sophisticated analyses (the data would clarify "volunteerism" when it is used as a dependent variable in conceptual or empirical research). This section offers some comments on the type of information that could be contained in such an inventory.

Information is available from several sources on the number of hours people spend volunteering, especially for formal organizations. Less information appears to be available on the amount of money and on the amount and type of goods they donate. For example, questions about money and goods were not asked in the National Longitudinal Surveys. In the 1973 Survey of Giving they were asked of a limited set of people; in other research the amount of a donation was not specified (as in the case of the 1981 Gallup study). Another neglected area seems to be informal donations of time, money, and goods. Although there are some data on the amount (in terms of time) and the kinds of unpaid labor that are donated to friends and neighbors, a complete picture would include data on the amount of informal donations of money and goods as well.

How donations of time, money, and goods are used is another issue that data collection might help to address. For instance, only a few sources document the extent to which people's volunteer time is devoted to (1) fund-raising events (so that others can be paid to do the work) and (2) the work directly (see, for example, the 1973 Survey of Giving and the 1981 Gallup). Less information is found on the ways in which donated goods are used, donations that range from old clothes given to Volunteers of America to residences left to universities after a person's death.

Another body of information concerns the timing of volunteerism. People volunteer during the weekdays, in the evenings and on weekends; they volunteer for short but concentrated periods of time and for longer, less intensive periods. Further, different types of activities seem to have different time arrangements. For example, participation in Little League activities occurs after school hours and is somewhat concentrated in time; donations to churches often occur once a week over the course of a year; and donations of time, money, and goods for Toys for Needy Children programs are concentrated in the holiday season. Detailed information on the timing of volunteerism in the form of unpaid labor specifically would improve estimates of the extent people trade off paid employment, homework, and leisure for volunteerism.

Finally, it has been mentioned that people are remunerated in different ways for their volunteering. Documenting the range of this variability could be useful if it can be proved more conclusively that people respond differently to different rewards. In addition, however, a special emphasis of data collecting should be the earnings of people who work for pay for organizations that rely on voluntary contributions. To the extent that these workers earn less than they could earn elsewhere, the pay differential is conceptually equivalent to a donation of money or time.

Motivations to Volunteer

Outlined below are some directions for research on the reasons why people volunteer. Four areas are considered: (1) the volunteer decision, (2) the amount and timing of volunteerism, (3) the interrelationship among the different ways people volunteer, and (4) the differences between formal and informal volunteering.

Some of the issues raised here could be investigated using the existing National Longitudinal Surveys cohort of older women. In 1974, 1976, and 1979, these women were asked a series of questions about their participation in formal volunteer organizations—the type of activity, the number of weeks per year and hours per week volunteered, and the type of positions held. Although this data base has been used extensively to address other issues, it has not been employed for investigations of volunteerism with the exception of this author's work.

The data set has a number of advantages: It is longitudinal and contains detailed information on the women's personal and family characteristics and their current and past work experiences, as well as some data on their attitudes toward, for example, work and appropriate roles for women. It also has some disadvantages—lack of information on donations of money and goods and the limited age/sex sample—but potentially these could be overcome. Also, additional questions could be added to future surveys of the same women, and the same questions could be asked in surveys of the other cohorts of the National Longitudinal Surveys: older men, younger men and women, and youth.[19]

The general approach of this research should be oriented toward policy. It should consider what factors motivate people to volunteer and which of these factors could be influenced by public policy to encourage greater participation in voluntary activities. The initial goal would be to understand whether people decide to volunteer and *then* select an activity or whether people decide to volunteer *for* particular activities. Past research suggests that people decide to volunteer for specific activities. If certain volunteer services are more urgently needed than others, it is important to understand what motivates people to volunteer for different activities in order to provide those particular services.

A reasonable hypothesis is that although people may be ready or willing to volunteer, they will actually volunteer only if they can choose their own activity; "being ready and willing" may be a necessary but not sufficient condition. As suggested by the literature review earlier in this paper, the sufficient condition may be a personal benefit that a volunteer derives from the activity. More work is needed to understand these motivations, work that uses the combined expertise of economists, sociologists, and psychologists.

This same issue exists for donations of money and goods. The existence of tax write-offs may make people willing to donate, but whether or not they do donate may depend upon the existence of organizations that meet some personal need or carry out some personal goal or belief. Although tax gains are one part of the compensation package, they are unlikely to comprise the entire package.

Another research issue—and an important policy area—concerns the amount and the timing of volunteerism. Alleviating or reducing some of society's problems, such as illiteracy and the medical needs of the elderly, will require a long-term effort; if volunteerism is to substitute for government expenditures and paid workers, then it must be sustainable over time. Such prolonged support could be achieved by relying on the same volunteers for long periods of time or by using an ever-changing work force of volunteers. But these "solutions" may in turn prove questionable. To the extent that volunteer organizations have high turnover among their volunteers, they will also require ongoing training and retraining capacities. This raises an organization's costs and thus reduces the efficiency with which it could carry out its activities. Analyses about the amount and timing of volunteerism would indicate whether continued reliance upon volunteers is an efficient way to provide services over long periods of time.

Data cited earlier indicate that few people volunteer year after year and that there is a broad range in the amount of time they donate. Also, casual observation suggests a greater willingness among people to do volunteer work for short, concentrated periods of time (such as in an emergency or during the holiday season) than for long, sustained periods. Or is this an illusion? Are the people who do the work during concentrated periods of time the same ones who volunteer over the course of a year? Alternatively, are there people who are only willing to volunteer at special times?

The amount of time people are willing to volunteer depends upon how much and what type of other activities they are willing to forgo—leisure pursuits, paid employment, or work inside the home. Similarly, for people to donate money or goods, they must be willing to give up alternative uses of that money and those goods. The amount and timing of a donation are likely to depend upon a household's income and the demands that are placed on it at different times of the year. For example, one could hypothesize that, among most families, sizable donations are unlikely to be made the day before a tax payment is due. Among low-income families in particular, even a small contribution is less likely to be made at Christmas or before school begins in the fall—times when there are desires and needs of one's own family to be met.

All of the discussion thus far on motivations has dealt with research that focuses on each form of volunteering (donations of time, money, and goods) individually. There is also a need for research that looks at these forms collectively and asks about their interrelationships. Do people interchange donations of money, time, and goods, or are these forms complementary?[23]

One way in which this issue is important is in the context of the increasing participation by women in the work force. Historically, the volunteer time of women has been a major part of volunteerism in America. But what happens when women move into paid employment? Do they continue their volunteer role to some extent, or do they change to giving money and goods?

One research result cited earlier was that the participation of women in the work force does not affect the likelihood that they will volunteer for social welfare or civic activities. This finding, which takes a cross-sectional view, is somewhat surprising; it goes against conventional wisdom. A next step would be to see if the finding holds in longitudinal analyses as well.

Another study might investigate the proposition—an implication of conventional wisdom about the impact of the movement of women into the work force—that a reduction in their volunteer time has negative consequences for volunteerism in general. Efficiency considerations suggest that a switch from donations of time (or goods) to greater donations of money actually may be preferable. Organizations can use money in any way (to buy stationery, pay workers, or purchase food, for instance) depending upon which resources are scarcer than others. In general, donated goods and time do not have this flexibility. Although an excess supply of goods can be sold to obtain money, this involves a transaction cost. Also, volunteers may not provide a stable work force (as mentioned earlier), and they may only be willing to undertake the more attractive tasks, leaving less desirable but still necessary ones unfinished.

The extent to which people interchange donations of time, money, and goods depends in part upon how volunteering time is viewed. If it is viewed as another form of work, a fair amount of substitution (donating money or goods rather than time) is likely to occur as women enter the labor force. Less substitution may occur if the volunteerism is viewed as a way of using leisure time.

Complicating the matter further, different volunteer activities may be viewed differently. High-status activities, such as heading a charity ball, may be considered leisure; lower-status activities, such as canvassing for the Heart Fund, may be more akin to work. This and previous discussions have focused on donations to formal volunteer organizations. There is evidence that participating in formal volunteer groups is largely a middle- and upper-class phenomenon. Does this imply that lower-income people are less likely to volunteer? Or do they volunteer more in casual, unstructured ways, such as helping friends and relatives or working for pay for formal volunteer groups?

In a more general vein, why do people help other people in informal ways? Are the reasons similar to those that lead people to volunteer in structured settings? A change in volunteerism from informal to formal settings may not have a significant impact on the amount of volunteerism if the same reasons hold. If the reasons differ, however, then a movement to more formal ways of volunteering may reduce the amount of volunteerism that occurs. It would be important to understand how society could compensate for such a decline.

One way of handling this question is to look to history. In the past many activities were carried out on an informal, sometimes ad hoc, basis. Some of these same activities—lending books and putting out fires, for example—are now handled within formal, organized systems (although informal volunteering is still with us; especially in times of emergency, people continue to band together, almost as a mutual insurance policy). Much of the past movement from informal to formal ways of carrying out activities may have been a response to increasing population densities and technological sophistication. Within a complex society there may be certain classes of problems that are more efficiently handled by formal, organized structures. Learning about these classes of problems in the context of historical changes in formal and informal volunteerism would help us understand more about the general direction volunteerism generally is likely to take in the future.

The Role of the Voluntary Sector

The research cited in this paper and the two previous sections on research questions have dealt with individuals and the circumstances under which they may volunteer. An equally important area for future work is the volunteer organization: the way it operates, the efficiency of its operations, and its organizational capacity. Volunteer organizations presumably have no profit motive; how then do they measure their own performances? And how do these measures affect their efficiency, that is, the way in which they distribute their own scarce resources? There is evidence that at least some volunteer organizations are notoriously inefficient and that only a small portion of the donations they receive are ever seen by the intended beneficiaries.

Further, from a historical perspective, how flexible have voluntary organizations been in adapting to changing social needs and circumstances? For example, to what extent have they adapted to the increasing participation of women in the work force? One response of these organizations might be to continue to rely on women who are not employed, an ever-shrinking pool. Another response might be to alter the timing of volunteering so that people could both work and volunteer.

A final broad area of research is the way in which the voluntary sector as a whole operates and the role it plays in the total economy.[24] On the one hand are social needs, and on the other freedom of choice among people to volunteer however they wish. It may be possible to rely upon these volunteers only for some social goals; in other areas, government expenditures and paid workers may be necessary.

Earlier sections of this paper suggest that the voluntary sector comprises thousands of individuals, all making separate decisions: whether or not to volunteer in the first place, what to volunteer for, what form the volunteerism should take, how much to do, and when to participate. This characterization suggests that the voluntary sector could be viewed as a "market for volunteerism." As in any market, there are people who supply the activity—the volunteers—and there are people who demand it—the beneficiaries of the volunteerism.

The key difference between this market and others, however, is that there is no pricing system in the volunteerism market. In other markets, prices serve a critical function; they determine the relative amount of each good that is both supplied and demanded. When high prices occur, more goods are supplied than may be demanded; in response, the supply declines and prices fall until an equilibrium price and quantity are established between those who demand goods and those who supply them.

Because there is no mechanism equivalent to a price system for regulating supply and demand within the voluntary sector, it is difficult to determine whether too little or too much of an activity is being supplied relative to demand (e.g., Are too many or too few Girl Scout cookies being sold?). The lack of a price system would not matter if resources were limitless. But in the voluntary sector, as elsewhere in the economy, resources are scarce and must somehow be allocated among competing uses.

It is quite probable that the suppliers of volunteerism do not systematically offer the range of goods and services that beneficiaries of volunteerism would like to be offered. And there are some goods that may not be produced if supply decisions are left solely to the workings of a marketplace. The beneficiaries of volunteerism must have a way of registering their demand so that a supply can be forthcoming. Normally, to demand a good requires having command over some resource (such as money) that can be traded; but in the case of the volunteerism market, the beneficiaries have no easy way of registering their demand. For example, we only know about the demand for food and shelter by the lines that form outside churches and other charitable organizations. Is this a sufficient measure of the demand for these services?

The volunteerism market may not generate the range of desired goods and services for another reason as well. As in other cases, it is likely that there are differences between the services that people, as individuals, are willing to supply themselves and those that they believe should be supplied as part of their social responsibility. For example, families may not be willing to house indigent persons themselves, but taken together they may wish such housing to be supplied. Identifying areas in which discrepancies such as this occur would suggest where governments could appropriately target their resources.

In sum, the supply of volunteerism, the demand for it, and the way in which voluntary contributions are allocated among competing social goals should be modeled both conceptually and empirically. Also, an understanding of the nature and extent of the differences between individually supplied and socially demanded services is a critical policy area. Because governments cannot solve all social ills, it is important to know where, and to what extent, they can rely upon the voluntary contributions of Americans.

CONCLUSIONS

Major changes are occurring within the American economy, changes that require increased volunteer activity. As a consequence of the reduction in expenditures of all levels of government, increasing demands are being placed on the voluntary sector to meet both immediate and long-term social needs. Furthermore, the aging of the population will lead to an increasing need for health care and other volunteer services for the elderly. The ways in which volunteers and volunteer organizations can, and will, respond to these changes are not really known. (For example, there is an expectation—or perhaps more accurately, a hope—that older, retired people will become a major source of volunteers. It may well be, however, that many individuals will not be eager to volunteer. Particularly if the retirement age continues to increase, they may prefer instead to relax and enjoy themselves after a lifetime of work.) Currently, little is understood about the extent and nature of volunteerism: the reasons why people volunteer, how they volunteer, and for what kind of activities they volunteer. Because of this information gap, it is not possible to suggest either ways to stimulate volunteerism in general or areas in which it is most likely to arise on its own.

It is also not quite clear whether an increase in volunteerism would be the most efficient way to supply needed services. How the voluntary sector allocates its own scarce resources remains obscure. We also do not know the extent to which the sector's activities do, or could, correspond to those that society at large considers valuable enough to undertake.

Today volunteerism is being promoted to meet social needs, a view that is based on assumptions about ways in which individuals could, or should, productively use their time. This view is also based on assumptions about the efficiency of the private voluntary sector as compared to the government sector in providing needed social services. It remains to be determined, however, whether people wish to use their time volunteering and whether volunteering is the most efficient means of achieving social goals.

*　　　　*　　　　*

Burkhard von Rabenau and Sara B. Toye provided helpful comments and suggestions on earlier drafts. The views expressed here are not necessarily those of the National Commission for Employment Policy or of the National Academy of Sciences and, of course, any errors are the author's.

NOTES

1. Gallup Organization, Inc., *Americans Volunteer*. Survey for Independent Sector (Princeton, N.J., June 1981).

2. ACTION, *Americans Volunteer, 1974* (Washington, D.C.: Independent Sector and the Gallup Organization, Inc., February 1975).

3. Carol L. Jusenius, *Retirement and Older Americans' Participation in Volunteer Activities* (Washington, D.C.: National Commission for Employment Policy, June 1983).

4. Ibid.

5. For a list of many of the ways in which people volunteer, see Gallup Organization, *Americans Volunteer*.

6. Gallup Organization, *Americans Volunteer*.

7. Jusenius, *Retirement and Older Americans' Participation*.

8. Kenneth Boulding, "Notes on a Theory of Philanthropy," in Frank Dickinson, ed., *Philanthropy and Public Policy* (New York: National Bureau of Economic Research, 1962).

9. Ibid., pp. 57, 61.

10. Gary S. Becker, "A Theory of Marriage: Part II," *Journal of Political Economy* 82, no. 3 (April 1974): S11–S26.

11. Marnie Mueller, "The Economic Determinants of Volunteer Work by Women," *Signs: Journal of Women and Society* 1, no. 4 (Winter 1975): 325–338; and Paul L. Menchik and Burton A. Weisbrod, "Government Crowding Out and Contributions of Time—Or Why do People Work for Free?" Unpublished paper. Dec. 8, 1982.

12. Mueller, "The Economic Determinants."

13. Other independent variables included husband's income, woman's current or last wage in the job market, youthfulness and number of children in the household, population size of the woman's place of residence, and woman's religion (Catholic, Protestant, Jew, or all other). The results of studies of these other independent variables indicated that women who identify with a religion and live in rural areas are likely to do more volunteer work than those who do not identify with a religion and live in urban areas.

14. Mueller, "The Economic Determinants," p. 334.

15. Menchik and Weisbrod, "Government Crowding Out," p. 5.

16. Ibid., p. 11. Other independent variables included measures of the population size of the person's place of residence; presence and age of children; the individual's age, sex, marital status, and income from other sources (such as interest and dividends); a measure of the amount of time the individual has spent helping friends and neighbors; and background characteristics of the individual (such as the parents' regular attendance at religious services, father's education, and regularity of parents' donations to charitable and religious organizations).

The results of the study indicated that more hours of volunteerism are undertaken by working people who live in larger rather than smaller cities, who are younger, and who give more help to friends and neighbors. For the area of natural resources specifically, working people with children in the family volunteer more hours than people without children; they volunteer fewer hours than those without children in the areas of education (all levels) and welfare.

17. Jusenius, *Retirement and Older Americans' Participation.*

18. Within this setting, household members' time can be conceptually divided into different activities. Some time is spent working to produce a household output of goods and services. This work is done both in the home and in the job market. For work done in the home, the compensation is the goods produced. For work done in the job market, the compensation is income, which can be used to buy goods and services in the market or to "buy time" to spend in activities other than work in the job market. For example, the income of one family member may be used to purchase household necessities as well as the time of a second family member so that he or she can be at home (taking care of children or taking early retirement).

Another part of household time is spent in leisure, the time devoted to consuming (or enjoying) the previously produced goods and services. More generally, leisure is time not working.

The statements above are a nontechnical description of the theory of the household's allocation of time. For technical versions, see Gary S. Becker, "A Theory of Marriage: Part I," *Journal of Political Economy* 81, no. 4 (July/Aug. 1973): 813–846; and Becker, "A Theory of Marriage: Part II."

19. The National Longitudinal Surveys sampled five separate cohorts: (1) men who were 45 to 59 years of age in 1966, (2) women who were 30 to 44 years of age in 1967, (3) young men aged 14 to 24 in 1966, (4) young women aged 14 to 24 in 1968, and (5) men and women aged 14 to 21 in 1979. In the first four cohorts blacks were oversampled so that they could be studied separately; there is about 15 years' worth of data for these groups. In the fifth cohort, "youth," whites from low-income households, blacks, and Hispanics were oversampled and persons in the military were included; these groups were most recently surveyed in 1982. For additional information, see the Center for Human Resource Research, *The National Longitudinal Surveys Handbook, 1982* (Columbus, Ohio: Center for Human Resource Research).

20. Independent variables included the individual's race, ethnicity (Latin or other origin), health status, employment status, place of residence and unemployment rate of that area, income from assets, and whether or not there were children in the household. For the women, an additional variable measured past participation in volunteer activities.

21. Menchik and Weisbrod, "Government Crowding Out."

22. This view was confirmed by program operators participating in a panel discussion entitled "Volunteerism: Can It Work in Your Community?" The panel was part of the 1982 Congress of Cities Exposition at Los Angeles, Nov. 27–Dec. 2, 1982.

23. For a further discussion of this issue, see, for example, James N. Morgan, Richard F. Dye, and Judith H. Hybels, "Results from Two National Surveys of

Philanthropic Activity," in *Research Papers, Volume I: History, Trends and Current Magnitudes,* sponsored by the Commission on Private Philanthropy and Public Needs (Washington, D.C.: U.S. Department of the Treasury, 1977).

24. For another way of conceptualizing the voluntary sector, the reader may wish to see Burton A. Weisbrod and Stephen H. Long, "The Size of the Voluntary Nonprofit Sector: Concepts and Measures," in *Research Papers.* Also, for empirical estimates of the size of the voluntary sector, see the Weisbrod and Long paper, others in that volume, and Burton A. Weisbrod, "Assets and Employment in the Nonprofit Sector," *Public Finance Quarterly* 10, no. 4 (Oct. 1982): 403–426.

The Older Volunteer Resource

Jarold A. Kieffer

The terms *older person, volunteer,* and *volunteer work* have acquired many different meanings in our society, a fact that causes confusion in discussing and interpreting data about the older volunteer. For instance, the 1981 Gallup survey on volunteerism in America used the "50 and older" category in identifying the age composition of the nation's volunteers.[1] In the same year the Louis Harris survey on aging focused on people over age 65 in asking its questions on volunteer activities. Other studies and documents discuss volunteer activity among people in the group aged 55 and over.[2]

Both in common usage and in studies of volunteerism the notion of volunteer work ranges from the unstructured help a person gives a bedridden neighbor to highly organized programs in which thousands of older people provide tax assistance to other older people on a volunteer basis. Some volunteer programs regard a volunteer only as someone who provides services without any type of monetary return—even one so small as the reimbursement of a bus trip or a meal. In other volunteer programs, reimbursements for out-of-pocket expenses are either a regular or a much-desired feature as an inducement in volunteer recruitment or retention.

Jarold A. Kieffer is a policy and management consultant.

In this paper, simply for the purpose of focusing discussion, the following will apply:

1. The terms *older people,* or *older person,* and *older volunteer* refer to people aged 55 and older.

2. *Volunteer work* is defined as full- or part-time employment with an organization (rather than on an individual, informal basis) for which no salaries, wages, or honoraria are received or expected, and for which no retirement, health insurance, or vacation or sick leave benefits are earned or granted. Also, the work done is not subject to the Social Security or Workers' Compensation tax and benefit systems. However, small stipends or reimbursements may be given for meals, travel, or other out-of-pocket expenses incurred in connection with the work done.

3. Service as a volunteer need not have a special linkage with certain types or classes of work. The term *volunteer work* is applied to any work activity that (a) could and might well be done for compensation but for some reason, at any given time, is not, or (b) is performed but probably would not be if, at a given time, the worker had to be paid. People who have paid jobs may do volunteer work in their spare time or on a released time basis, the latter on the basis of an agreement with their employers.

4. The possibilities for expanding the role of older volunteers are examined from the standpoint of public policy, employers, unions, paid workers, and older people. Many questions and issues that have been raised in connection with the possible expanded use of older volunteers are really part of the larger issue of the expanded use of volunteers of all ages in our society. However, some special questions and issues do attach to the expanded use of older volunteers, and that (rather than the general subject of volunteerism) is the focus of this paper.

THE NEED AND THE OPPORTUNITY

At all levels of American life, social service and many other types of program managers are finding that their financial resources are shrinking while their workloads continue to grow. Federal grants-in-aid for many services performed in our communities have been declining because of reductions in appropriations or inflation or both. Budget problems and inflation also are forcing many states and localities to reduce the funds they can provide for such programs, and business difficulties and tax changes are limiting the funds that businesses pay in taxes or contribute to private and voluntary organizations that furnish services. Some foundation-assisted programs also have had to be curtailed because of smaller amounts of money available for philanthropy.

Personnel costs tend to be the most expensive category in the budgets of service organizations. Consequently, budget-cutting efforts are forcing personnel reductions that result either in whole ranges of service being eliminated or in services being maintained but on a reduced or lower quality basis. No doubt such service reductions will have long-term consequences that will prove costly in human and dollar terms, but these costs tend to be hard to calculate. Therefore, their overall scope is rarely identified and reflected in public and private sector budgets. Instead, society pays the costs in year-by-year increments through its often belated efforts to cope with underemployment, unemployment, fear, insecurity, crime, isolation, poor health, dependency, community decay, lost business profits, and lower property values.

The growing numbers of able older people could be a major resource in easing the impact of personnel cuts that lead to reductions in social service and other types of service agencies. Already numbering about 50 million, the older population is expected to grow to more than 53 million by the end of this decade and to nearly 60 million by the end of the century. Of the current older population (figures as of 1984), over 68 percent of those between ages 55 and 64 and 88 percent of those over age 65 are no longer counted in the work force (in 1970, the corresponding figures were 61 percent and 83 percent). Some of these people, mostly women, were in the work force only for short periods; others have retired or are classified as discouraged workers who are no longer counted as currently seeking work.

The 1981 Louis Harris study estimated that about 5.9 million, or 23 percent, of the population over age 65 "performed some voluntary service." The 1981 Gallup survey of the same age group stated that its calculations showed that 9.6 million, or 37 percent, claimed that they did volunteer work. The Gallup figures, however, included both organized, formal volunteer activity and informal, individual activity.[3] Edmund Worthy summarized the 1981 Harris survey data on the volunteer activity of people over age 65:

- three-fifths are women, two-fifths are men;
- 92 percent are white, 6 percent are black, and 2 percent are Hispanic;
- 43 percent are aged 65 to 69, 46 percent are aged 70 to 79, and 11 percent are aged 80 or older;
- almost 33 percent are college graduates, slightly more than a third finished high school and had some college work, and about a third did not graduate from high school;
- 25 percent had incomes over $20,000, 25 percent had incomes between $10,000 and $20,000, 25 percent had incomes between $5,000 and $10,000, and 25 percent had incomes under $5,000; and
- volunteerism among people over age 65 who are still in the work force appears to be declining, although it is increasing among people over age 65 who have retired.[4]

THE CURRENT AND POTENTIAL OLDER VOLUNTEER POOL

The 1981 Harris survey also sought to learn whether older nonvolunteers had an interest in volunteering. The response indicated that 1 in 10 had such an interest (about 2.55 million people in the population over age 65 in 1981). Worthy noted that this 2.55 million added to the 5.9 million people in the same age group who said they were now doing volunteer work might mean that about 8.5 million people over age 65 could be considered to be the current and potential volunteer pool in that age category.

Turning to volunteerism among the people in the group aged 55 to 64, the 1981 Gallup survey found that 45 percent (or 9.8 million) of the people in this age group said that they did volunteer work; the Hamilton survey figure was 31 percent (or 6.7 million). Given the very liberal definition of volunteer work used by Gallup, the Hamilton figure might be the safer one to use.

Gallup did not present figures on nonvolunteers aged 55 to 64 who said that they were interested in volunteering. But Hamilton found that 26 percent of the 15 million nonvolunteers aged 55 to 64 (or 3.9 million) said that they would be interested.

These estimates suggest that the current and potential pool of volunteers drawn from people 55 years and older is as follows:

Age Group	Persons Now Volunteering (millions)	Persons Interested in Volunteering (millions)	Totals[a] (millions)
55 to 64	6.7	3.90	10.60
65 and older	5.9	2.55	8.45
Totals	12.6	6.45	19.05

[a]These are 1981 estimates. By 1990, the pool could include several million more older people.

No ready basis exists for judging either the number of additional older volunteers needed or the number who actually would respond to an expanded call for their help on a voluntary basis. We do know from the Harris survey that many older people feel involuntarily idled through forced and premature retirement; indeed, many do not feel fully occupied even though they are still working. Others retired voluntarily but came later to realize that they did not have a sense of clear purpose to keep them active and motivated day by day.

Older women form a group of varying abilities and changing patterns of volunteerism. Some older women who have not sought to rejoin the work force are past the point of having daily concerns with growing children and household responsibilities. In terms of volunteering, many of these women have skills and experience that could be used at once in a wide variety of social service organizations; others would need training or skill updating; and still others would need extensive training and counseling or could be used only in low-skill capacities. Older women traditionally have been a major source of volunteers. But, in the past 15 years, changes in the family status of many women, inflation, and new views on women's roles have sharply reduced the pool of women aged 45 to 65 who are still willing to give time to volunteer work. Some organizations that depend upon female volunteers have had losses of between 25 and 40 percent over the last five years. Retired or near retired men and women could be a natural group to help make up these losses.

IMPEDIMENTS TO THE OLDER VOLUNTEER

The table presented earlier indicates that nearly 6.5 million people aged 55 and older might be interested in doing volunteer work. But even if we are conservative in judging what people actually will do as against what they say they might do and reduce the figure to, say, 4 million, it is still difficult to predict whether volunteers in anything like these numbers will come forward. Without a clearer understanding of what makes people volunteer, we are left with "It all depends . . ."

There is a need for many more older volunteers, and older persons have the availability and capacity to meet this need; these points are clear. Yet why are these people still so generally neglected? Are the problems or impediments to volunteering mostly in the minds of older individuals, or are they in the habits of thinking and action of the people in the organizations that might seek their help? As might be expected, both older people themselves and the organizations for which they might volunteer have contributed to the current situation. Indeed, although the idea and value of expanding the number of older volunteers may seem to be self-evident, an expansion initiative has not as yet attracted important leadership, in either the public or private sectors. Some of the elements of this situation are described next.

President Ronald Reagan (and earlier Presidents) and many private sector leaders have encouraged greater voluntary efforts in our society. But they have tended to say very little to encourage and challenge large numbers of older people to volunteer. Also—and this is of critical importance—they have not identified and taken actions to clear away obstacles to older volunteer recruitment and retention. Although the 1981 White House Conference on Aging and a number of national advisory groups in the past several years have urged greater attention to the older person as a continuing resource, little response has developed, in either the public or private sectors, to expanding recruitment and retention of older people as volunteers. The Reagan administration also has not increased the size of several small, older-volunteer programs that it inherited. And Congress has not moved in this area or in attempting to provide more incentives to volunteer. Federal and some state tax codes allow limited expense deductions for people who volunteer, but these deductions tend to help people who have high enough incomes to benefit from deductions. Large numbers of older people are not in this category.

In fact, our society has been systematically writing off the skills, capacities, and experience of older people since the end of World War II. It is not surprising, therefore, that no sudden exception is made now to proclaim the valuable contributions older people can make as volunteers.

Another facet of the problem involves the unions. Labor unions commonly are suspicious and fearful about the use of volunteers of any age in many categories of paid employment. Government workers' unions, in particular, believe that volunteerism could be exploited by public agencies to displace paid workers. Their concerns have been heightened by high rates of joblessness and extensive layoffs at the same time that the President has been calling for a broader emphasis on volunteerism. (Some governors and mayors also have been talking about the broader use of volunteers to help offset staff cuts forced by budget reductions.) Because of these fears on the part of workers, many public employers who otherwise might be supportive of the broader use of volunteers (of all ages) tend to hesitate about moving in this direction. They are reluctant to antagonize the public worker and other unions and the families and friends of union members.

Like older people who work for pay or seek paying jobs, older persons actually serving as volunteers or looking for such assignments face many of the same kinds of age discrimination and discouragement policies and practices in the workplace. Such policies and practices are often found in organizations that commonly employ volunteers.

Another impediment to a greater use of older persons as volunteers may be that older people themselves are divided on the subject of their volunteerism. Some are dubious about accepting what they perceive to be the second class status they feel often attaches to volunteer work. Others who feel that more opportunities should be provided for older people to work for pay reason this way: If volunteerism gets a higher priority among policymakers, then policymakers will tend to give less attention to expanding paid work opportunities.

The Gallup, Harris, and Hamilton surveys show clearly that people who have low incomes tend to volunteer less than people who have more income. One of the difficulties may be that volunteers often need money for transportation and meals. Although some organizations reimburse volunteers for such costs, many are not able to do so. And the limited financial resources of some older people do not permit them the luxury of being out-of-pocket for a few days or weeks until they can be reimbursed.

Older people also say that, beyond the rising costs of transportation as an impediment to their doing volunteer work, they do not have adequate means to move about. Many can no longer afford to own, repair, and insure automobiles, and they do not want to be dependent upon others for their movement. In addition, many older people have become afraid to drive or go on buses or subways because their vision is poor, because they fear criminals, or because they do not wish to stand on street corners or in stations waiting for buses or subways. Higher costs are also forcing transit operators to reduce services in many communities, which is also hurting the ability of many people, including the elderly, to get to and from places of interest to them. Finally, public transit throughout the nation has failed to find adequate means of providing services to most of the people who live and work in the vast suburban areas that surround our old central cities. Many people now in their upper 50s and 60s bought homes or rented in these suburbs, and increasingly they are cut off from many pursuits because of inadequate transportation.

Older people sometimes stay away from volunteer work, using the excuses of poor health or lack of time, when they are actually feeling "burned-out" or "turned-off." After lifetimes of work and contending with their own concerns, some people do not wish to become involved in activities that might entangle them with other people's problems. (This response is exactly the opposite to that of people who like to focus on other people's problems in order to cope with their own problems, for instance, inactivity, isolation, or loss of purpose.) In other cases, older people resist the impulse or hesitate to become volunteers because they are skeptical about the value of what they would be doing or because they no longer feel they could tolerate bureaucratic practices. They fear demeaning assignments that other older volunteers have told them they can expect to receive. Or they do not wish to be placed under professional (and especially younger) supervisors, individuals they judge to be lacking in understanding about life and survival.

In many organizations that do use or could use volunteers, a curious split-level kind of thinking often impedes effective actions to encourage more volunteer recruitment and retention. In such cases, the organization's leaders may pay lip service to volunteerism, but elements of the professional and clerical staffs may have negative perceptions about volunteers. These individuals see all volunteers (but perhaps especially older volunteers) as often unreliable because they seem to give higher priority to their own affairs and needs (when it suits them) than to those of the organization. Professional staff often complain that volunteers come in and leave whenever they want, lay down conditions on their availability that conflict with the needs of their supervisors, and yet demand high-status jobs and recognition. These behaviors lead professionals to conclude that volunteers cannot be counted on to carry important responsibilities and should be given only less sensitive roles.

Professional staff members also tend to consider volunteers unruly and beyond effective discipline. They say volunteers want to do things their own way and often complain about the alleged inadequacies of professional staff and the plans they make or orders they give. Further complaints by professionals are that volunteers bother and take the valuable time of supervisors and other staff, require space and other support (and complain when they do not get it), and mill around or get in the way because they are often present when they are not needed. It is not an exaggeration to state that paid staff in many organizations have an acquired professional bias against volunteers and often feel compelled to express their negative feelings to those volunteers.

The professional bias impediment has growing significance, because many private and voluntary organizations that traditionally use volunteers are becoming more professionalized in their staffing. More and more often, professional staff are being inserted between volunteer governing board members and volunteers who make up the rank and file workers of organizations. In addition, when paid professional vacancies develop, the "inside" professionals tend to pick as replacements other professionals from inside or outside the organizations involved; they seldom fill the positions from among the inside volunteers who might aspire to a paid job. This process has been taking hold for some years, and, as a result in many organizations the role of volunteers and their relationships to organizational leaders and professional staffs are now becoming vague. Also, some of these organizations neglect or do not have effective policies on the roles of volunteers and their advancement or recognition, a growing gap that is reflected later in progressively less effective programs and action for the recruitment, training, and use of volunteers. Not unexpectedly, these conditions, in a circular way, then lead to circumstances in which volunteers become out of touch, ill-informed on organizational priorities, and dissatisfied. Indeed, in such circumstances they become people who may be around but who are definitely in the way.

WHAT CAN BE DONE?

Corrective measures could be taken in the following areas (each of which is developed in detail later in this section):

- positive appeal to older people and strengthened recruitment;
- improved efforts and means for older volunteer recognition;
- improved supervision, development, and management of volunteer programs; and
- removal or reduction of specific impediments to older volunteer recruitment and retention efforts.

As will be seen, these proposed measures are highly interactive. Each action, if taken effectively, could be helpful in reinforcing the other actions proposed.

Positive Appeal to Older People and Strengthened Recruitment

Many reasons were given earlier in this paper for the failure to develop major efforts in the recruitment and retention of older volunteers, despite the obvious resource they could be for meeting the growing workload problems of social service and other types of service organizations. Yet the 1981 Harris survey suggests that a common reason given by older people for their noninvolvement is that no one really asked them. This response actually has three aspects. The first is the difference between coming forward—volunteering on the basis of one's own initiative—and being asked to volunteer. The second has to do with the need for specialized appeals to older people as distinguished from general calls for volunteers. The third involves the content and methods of specialized appeals to older people.

Many older people have become adept over the years at identifying and avoiding situations they feel would be unpleasant. Also, many older people have learned, through long experience, to discount blandishments and sales talk. Yet older people usually are not much different from people of other ages in the way they react to special personal and flattering attention. When someone, especially someone known to and respected by them, personally asks for their help, they are more likely to respond affirmatively than they would if the appeal were nonpersonal or made by someone not known to them. Their egos and even their guilt feelings may then overcome their reasons for hesitation or refusal. Perhaps the personal recruiting effort for older people may have to be more intensive than is needed for younger people, but its dynamics and outcomes are quite similar. Some of the religious organizations have employed these volunteer recruiting approaches with success for years.

This type of appeal will require a major change in the current volunteer recruitment practices of many organizations. Apart from the need to make recruiting more personalized, they will also have to make a special point of recruiting older people. Organizations such as the American Association of Retired Persons, the National Council on the Aging, the National Council of Senior Citizens, and ACTION (a federal agency) have tried for several years to bring attention to the older person as a valuable volunteer resource. Some interest is growing, but the fact remains, as noted earlier, that most organizations using volunteers have not yet actively sought to recruit large numbers of older people.

What is needed is a major effort by the President and by other public and private sector leaders to urge organizations to gain the special strengths of older people as volunteers and to draw the attention of older people to the opportunities for volunteering and the nation's special need for their help. Such top-level leadership efforts need to be well publicized and continued over a period of time. In addition to appealing to older people through the media, other methods must be used: special messages in stores, senior residences, recreation centers, libraries, churches, restaurants, service clubs and associations, and other places where older people gather. Printed appeals can be helpful, but follow-up is also necessary both through networks of older people who can reach each other at the community level and through direct appeals to older people at their gatherings.

Private employers can help older volunteer recruitment through counseling older workers, donating funds for recruitment efforts and publicity, and "loaning" older employees to organizations needing volunteers (employees can be given time off or recognition for volunteer service). Some employers already do these things, but more need to be brought into the effort. Also, some employers might be willing to donate money to service organizations in proportion to an hourly rate for the time their employees work for these organizations on their own time.

Beyond the methodologies of recruitment efforts is the content of recruitment. The message is critical, especially since older people are quite used to the idea that their skills and experience are not highly valued and that they are likely to be given low-ranking tasks if they are accepted as volunteers. If an organization that uses volunteers means to attract older volunteers, it will find that it must relegate age to the background as a job- or duty-limiting factor. Older people are probably more aware than anyone that the great majority of individuals in their age group are still physically and mentally able. Even many of those who have muscle weaknesses, stiffness in some joints, and some diminishment of vision and hearing can still do many kinds of physical and mental tasks. Most can manage, plan, write, talk, drive, ride, walk, cajole, assemble, use calculators, press buttons, and so on. These people want to feel that they will be given duties that are challenging to them, meaningful to the public and to the volunteer organization, and, above all, truly helpful in dealing with individual and community problems.

Many older people will respond better to recruitment efforts if they know that the organization they join will see them as individuals who have skills, experience, and continuing aspirations. With the earlier retirements and longer life expectancies likely in the years ahead, many more older people will perceive that they can have new careers after they retire from their original careers. For some, the way to move toward a new career will be to start as a volunteer in an organization that is doing something of interest to them or that will permit them to learn or practice skills that later can command a salary or wages. They will want to be regarded as still trainable and capable of assuming larger responsibilities if they can demonstrate growth capacities. For some older people these things are not as important as finding a congenial work atmosphere, including the chance to be with old friends or to make new ones. If asked to volunteer, these people will want to be assured that their part of the work is valuable to the mission of the organization and that they are not being exploited as someone's drudge. In this case, the organization must actually deliver on its recruitment promises. If it does not, its recruiting credibility will be undercut quickly by the effective word-of-mouth communication that exists among older people.

Improved Recognition and Appreciation

Closely related to recruiting is the degree to which organizations project themselves as solicitous of good morale among their workers. Unpaid volunteers probably will not stay involved long if their morale is poor. Older volunteers are not unlike volunteers of other ages in their need for recognition and appreciation. If anything, older people may feel more need to be recognized because they know that they face declining opportunities for their families, friends, and associates to see how their work and efforts are still appreciated and rewarded.

Recognition has other values to older volunteers. For those who have been out of organized work for a long time or who are participating in new types of activities as volunteers, commendation and recognition provide a sense of performance evaluation and the encouragement to do more. Recognition can also reassure the family members of older volunteers, who sometimes feel that organizations may be exploiting their older relatives. Recognition award ceremonies allow the families to become more acquainted with the volunteer organization and what it does; they can then feel proud of their parent or grandparent for doing such useful things.

Volunteerism is highly valued in the abstract in American society. Yet many people have the notion that volunteers are considered second-class workers—and treated that way—even in many volunteer organizations. Furthermore, when listed in a resume, volunteer activities seem to be lightly regarded and indeed are often discounted. This is not surprising in a society that tends to equate the work value and importance of people with the compensation they receive. Retired people especially are aware of how their sense of worth declines when they retire and how other people tend to downgrade the importance of a person who is retired. Some of this same kind of depreciation is sensed by older people when they say they are doing volunteer work.

One way to help offset these problems would be to encourage organizations that employ volunteers to develop simulated or imputed budgets that estimate the value of the work done by volunteers and the compensation they would get if they were paid. In fact, organizations should assign dollar values to all of the in-kind services or other donated help they receive. These figures should then be incorporated as a special chapter in their published budgets and annual reports. Bringing these figures to light will enable boards of directors, staffs, volunteers, and public and private sector policymakers, as well as the public, to gain a better perspective on the real value of donated work and services and how they figure in the total story of what organizations do and what their services really cost.

Imputed budgets such as these also help volunteers calculate their financial value to the organizations they serve. Using imputed budgets, they and their employers and the professional staffs of the organizations would see at a glance what would be lost if the volunteer force disappeared. Volunteers could then assign a dollar value to their work in the salary/wage-history portion of their resumes or when they are talking to prospective employers (for paid or other volunteer work) or to friends and family.

Improved Supervision, Development, and Management

All volunteers need a sense of purpose and direction. They also must feel that they and what they do are highly valued by their employing organization and by the public. Older people are more likely than younger people to become impatient quickly with weak organizational arrangements for volunteers and to speak out or walk away. Then, too, many older people tend to have higher expectations about the value of their skills and experience and the expenditure of their time. Some enter volunteer work with the idea that they should be given responsibilities that involve prestige, scope, and discretion to act. In many cases this is not possible, and both the organizations and the older volunteers become mutually frustrated and antagonistic. Probably one of the most difficult but also one of the most common situations is the placement of older volunteers under the administrative and program supervision of much younger professionals. Usually both parties are at an extreme disadvantage, and often friction and destructive tension result.

There are no easy formulas either to avoid or to remedy these problems. Some useful preventive as well as "damage control" ideas have been assembled by the national volunteer support organizations. Although some of these ideas are intended to help deal with situations involving volunteers of all ages, those outlined below would have particular utility in organizational relationships with older volunteers.

Some volunteers can give a limited amount of time; others can be on the job day in and day out. It is important, therefore, that organizations not lump all volunteers together in one category when assessing the level and type of responsibilities to which they could be assigned. People of ability and great experience who can devote considerable time to the organization could, in many cases, be treated as regular staff members, except that they do not receive pay and fringe benefits. Too often, volunteers—because they are volunteers—are denied this treatment. In many organizations, stiff rules, often developed as a result of court decisions on liability, prevent volunteers from being able to serve in a line capacity or make commitments that bind the organization or its funds. Lack of compensation appears to be the only factor that bars the volunteer from doing these things. Therefore, one suggestion is that organizations explore and gain legal acceptance of the concept of deputization. Under this concept, the organization agrees to allow a volunteer to perform certain duties specified in writing. The volunteer accepts these responsibilities but declines compensation. The organization accepts liability for what the volunteer does and regards him or her as an employee for liability insurance or other legal purposes. Most organizations would not need to deputize many volunteers, but the arrangement would allow the organization greater flexibility in taking advantage of the skills and experience of volunteers. For people who do not need or want compensation, the arrangement permits them to be helpful without needless and arbitrary restrictions on what they may do to be helpful.

The deputization idea has the further advantage that it can be used for varying lengths of time, such as for a day, week, month, or whatever temporary period is appropriate.

Far too often the professionals and volunteers in an organization face each other over an invisible but thick wall that tends to degrade the volunteers, discourage the fullest use of their skills and experience, and deny them a sense of creative participation in shaping, carrying out, and evaluating the effectiveness of what the organization does. Creative participation requires involvement. Organizations need to imbue volunteers with the sense that they—the volunteers—are genuinely involved in thinking through their organization's problems, opportunities, and priorities. This can be done by a continuous process of briefing and debriefing, plus think sessions in which facts, ideas, and constraints are all exposed for mutual consideration and reaction. The process takes time, but it pays dividends in terms of improved performance and morale. It is especially important for volunteers to be able to make suggestions as to the best ways they can be employed on organizational tasks and for their suggestions to be given careful consideration and follow-up if that is merited.

Volunteers should be given a sense of motion once they enter the organization and begin their work. This includes careful training in understanding their expected duties and the mission and character of the organization. Experienced volunteers should be encouraged to help shape and provide such training. Volunteers also should be encouraged to feel that they can move up in the level of responsibilities they carry. While organizations cannot always find among the volunteers the skills they need in their paid staff, volunteers who wish to have a paid job should be encouraged to apply, if they feel they are qualified, to fill vacancies.

Some organizations are developing job descriptions for their volunteer jobs. Such descriptions, if brief and clear, can help the volunteer understand both his or her own duties and also clarify the relationships between fellow volunteers, paid staff, and supervisory levels up the line. Beyond the importance of helping volunteers know who does what, organizations should give them a chance to fill various jobs over time. This process gives them an opportunity to learn more about what the organization does, and it gives them a way to demonstrate that they can learn new things and grow in skill and experience.

Despite some natural antipathies, professional staff and volunteers must learn to rely on each other and work together. Ensuring such an outcome has to be one of the principal tasks of organizational leaders. Suggestions have been made above for improving some of the substantive aspects of these relationships, but attention must be given to the matter at the logistical or support levels as well. For instance, volunteers must know exactly what help they can get from paid clerical staff—the "ground rules" must not be left to chance. Organizations have to recognize that the use of volunteers has costs, but effective logistical support of volunteers pays continuous dividends. Clerical staff must be carefully briefed on how to deal responsively with volunteers who need help with typing, supplies, space, reimbursements, and directions on where to find people, equipment, forms, and other items necessary to their work. Some organizations try to centralize staff responsibilities for meeting the logistics requirements of volunteers to avoid situations in which the clerical staff is placed under pressure from many sources at the same time. Other organizations prefer to decentralize these responsibilities and assign them to administrative assistants of the various divisions. The main idea, however, is still to channel volunteer demands and arrange for their needs with some sense of divisional priority. The reaction of clerical staff can be critical in these arrangements. An arrogant or negative secretary or administrative assistant can create an atmosphere in the offices of an organization that directly undercuts the image it seeks to project to its volunteers. Here, too, the problems and opportunities relate to volunteers of all ages, but, older volunteers might well be less patient in confronting unsatisfactory logistical conditions and make comments that add to tensions. Or—the last resort—they may give up on the organization.

Removal or Reduction of Impediments to Older Volunteers

Legal Restrictions

The federal government and some states and localities operate under laws or rules that sharply restrict the use of volunteers.[5]

Such restrictions have developed from fears that the use of unpaid workers could lead to such problems as favoritism, non-professionalism, political intrusion, financial manipulation, and confusion. Also, government workers' unions have feared that the use of volunteers could deprive people of paid work opportunities. These possibilities cannot be disregarded. All of these problems actually occurred at one time or another at various levels of government, and the restrictions have been given the force of law to ensure that they will not happen again.

Now, however, new circumstances are arising. Many public services that the public has become accustomed to having or that it must have are being reduced because of unprecedented and currently unmanageable deficits that are confounding efforts to restore the health of the economy. The list of critical individual and community needs left unmet is growing, and these unmet needs have been added to many that already existed before budgetary concerns became so compelling to policymakers at all levels and in both political parties. Under these conditions the public policy issue to be weighed is an assessment of risk: whether the risks that might be run in expanding the use of volunteers in government agencies, or in expanding the use of more private and voluntary agencies to substitute for government agencies in performing some public or public-supported services, are greater than the risks (including the short- and long-term costs) of failing to perform these services. If enough money is not voted by legislatures at all levels to enable governments to provide mandated and other important services and program leaders cannot hire or retain adequate staff to keep their programs running effectively, should they be left with no options other than to cut out more services or further dilute those still provided?

Current legal and other restrictions on the use of volunteers in government programs need review. Also, there should be further study of the confusing cost data that have been used in both sides of the argument on the use of nongovernmental units (both for-profit and not-for-profit) to perform services now performed by governments. Substantial numbers of capable older people are available to help the nation cope with its growing crisis of unmet needs. It should be possible to open up more opportunities for these people to serve as volunteers in providing services of many types and at the same time protect the public against abuses and avoid casual and unwarranted displacement of paid workers.

Expenses

Another impediment to volunteering by some low- and middle-income older people is that they cannot afford out-of-pocket expenses for fuel, parking, food, and sometimes even clothing in connection with work as a volunteer. No estimate can be made of how serious this problem may be. However, the subject keeps appearing on lists of reasons people offer as to why they do not come forward as volunteers, and many older people are too proud to admit that this is a problem for them. The national volunteer support organizations say it is a considerable problem for would-be volunteers. Organizations often see the problem in a very practical way. Current or would-be volunteers ask if expenses can be reimbursed, and the organizations in many cases have to refuse because they do not have the funds. The organizations then find that many of these people do not return.

Some organizations have been able to find the funds to offer small grants to volunteers for their expenses. Many more have been unsuccessful, and the deepening funding problems they are experiencing because of the recession suggest that this situation may not change. It could even get worse for those organizations that do provide expenses. Some of the federal older volunteer programs have been providing small grants to reimburse their volunteers for expenses, but the total federal volunteer group is very small.[6]

Support and Encouragement

Some older people, once they have decided to volunteer, will need special attention on the job. Often older people have been out of organized activities for a long time, and they may not be used to working closely with others, to working under supervision, or to meeting deadlines. Some will not have participated in training of any kind for decades; still others may doubt their endurance and their capacity to work long periods. Organizations that have volunteer programs can structure their training programs to alert professional staff and other volunteers to the worries and doubts that some older volunteers will have. Recognition of this issue by the staff and other volunteers and quiet help and encouragement can go a long way in easing these people through possibly difficult orientation periods.

Liability Insurance

If a volunteer (of any age) gets hurt or hurts someone while doing volunteer work, who is liable—the volunteer, the organization, or both? Some organizations have liability insurance to cover themselves for both possibilities. However, this insurance, although decreasing in cost, is still an expensive item for organizations that use large numbers of volunteers. For this reason most organizations do not protect their volunteers and often do not protect themselves. In some cases the organizations advise volunteers that they must bear personal responsibility for their actions. Many, however, say nothing about the subject for fear of discouraging people from volunteering.

This matter is beginning to concern more and more organizations, but they are divided as to courses of action. Some fear that if they begin buying liability coverage, lawyers will see it as an invitation to test how far they can go in collecting damages. And the whole question of liability has not yet been seen as a major impediment to the recruiting of volunteers. Some allegations are made that the issue could become more important if substantial numbers of older people are attracted to volunteer work. This kind of thinking squares with the commonly held belief that older people have more accidents, are subject to more lapses that could result in other people being injured, and when hurt have more serious problems that are costly to treat. Such thinking probably will change only if more organizations experiment with the recruitment of much larger forces of older volunteers and factual data can be developed on the comparative rates of younger and older volunteers who have accidents or hurt others.

The voluntary organizations consider the liability subject to be a gray area that needs careful study and consideration. Most realize that they are operating "at risk," and that the whole voluntary community could one day wake up to find some court decisions that have awarded major damages to someone hurt by a volunteer on duty. The organizations also may find that even some of those that currently carry liability insurance on some of their volunteer leaders are not protected from the actions of their lower-ranking volunteers while on duty.

Age Bias

The greatest impediment to a major expansion in the numbers of older volunteers is bias against the elderly. Its mitigation will depend upon individual leadership in organizations that use volunteers and among older people themselves. These leadership efforts could be aided by the development of new data or better interpretation of available data on the capacities of older people to learn to adjust, perform skills, and avoid accidents. But gaining solid performance data on older workers has been increasingly difficult, at least on a current and acceptably large enough scale, because our society has assumed for years that older people were supposed to leave the work force and therefore were not worth observing for testing purposes. The reduction in the number of people over age 55 in the work force continues, and now some believe that the small remnant of this population still working is not representative of the older population and its performance capacities.

The means must be developed for conducting large-scale demonstrations of the capacities and performance of older workers. Otherwise, our society will not break out of the present circular process wherein we witness the massive departure of older people from the workplace and then say that there are no longer enough older people working to justify the conclusion that most older people could still perform effectively in our economy. The encouragement of further inquiry, of a search for new knowledge, and of better interpretation of available data in this area—accompanied by the articulation of research, interpretation, and demonstration needs—could be a major contribution by the Institute of Medicine.

NOTES

1. Gallup Organization, Inc., *American Volunteer.* Survey for Independent Sector (Princeton, N.J., 1981).

2. Louis Harris and Associates, Inc. "Aging in the Eighties: America in Transition." Study for the National Council on the Aging, Inc. (Washington, D.C., 1981); Hamilton and Staff, Inc., "Older Americans and Volunteerism." Survey for the Program Division of the National Retired Teachers Association/American Association for Retired Persons (Washington, D.C., 1981); "Older Americans: An Untapped Resource." Study prepared for the National Committee on Careers for Older Americans, Academy for Educational Development, Inc. (New York, N.Y., 1979).

3. Gallup Organization, Inc., "Americans Volunteer."

4. Edmund H. Worthy, "Older Volunteers: Profiles and Prospects." Paper presented at the Eighth Annual Meeting of the Association for Gerontology in Higher Education, Feb. 12, 1982. In this paper, Worthy summarized both the published and unpublished parts of the 1981 Harris survey (see note 2) relating to the views of older respondents about volunteer activities. He also provided independent analysis of the

Harris data. See also a later paper by Worthy and Catherine Venture Merkel, "Older Volunteers: A Fact Sheet" (Washington, D.C.: National Council on the Aging, Inc., 1982).

5. Limitation on Voluntary Services, 31 U.S.C. .L1342. This provision developed from a section of the Budget and Accounting Act of 1921. Section 1342 has been amended to permit greater latitude in the use of youth volunteers and the provision of expense stipends to them.

In 1982 Representative Mickey Edwards (a Republican from Oklahoma) introduced H.R. 1323, the Volunteers in Government Act. The bill would authorize greater freedom to federal agency heads to use volunteers. Comparable bills were introduced in the Senate, but major support for the bills failed to develop.

Also in that Congress, Representative Panetta of California introduced H.R. 1264, which would have authorized the creation of a Select Committee on Voluntary Service to study ways of encouraging more volunteerism and make reports to the Congress on ways to remove impediments. The bill mentioned older people as a resource for voluntary agencies but did not emphasize this aspect of volunteer potential.

6. "The Office of the Older American Volunteer Programs, a part of ACTION—the national volunteer agency—includes three programs: the Foster Grandparent Program, the Senior Companion Program, and the Retired Senior Volunteer Program. Together, these programs involve 323,310 volunteers, 60 years or older. They serve 1,042 local projects and devote an annual total of 75,768,484 hours of service to their local communities" (from "*ACTION News* Older American Volunteer Programs Fact Sheet"; information current as of April 1982).

Unpaid Productive Activity Over the Life Course

James N. Morgan

We all start life being dependent on others, net recipients of goods and services. Then, after an extended period of productive activity, some of it paid for in money, we once again consume more than we produce, although we may well have saved enough to pay for most or all of that consumption. Much is known about people's paid work, both about their earnings and their hours of work. The rapid increase of paid work by women, even those with small children to care for, has been studied thoroughly. It is clear that as a society we are at some kind of peak in terms of the aggregate amount of productive time available in relation to the population. Even without a resurgence in births, as the baby-boom generations reach retirement age we shall have fewer paid workers and probably fewer aggregate paid work hours available relative to the total population to be fed, clothed, and housed.

These factors put unpaid work—particularly the possibility of more mutual and self-help among the elderly in our population—in a new perspective. Unfortunately, because there are no markets, no official records, and no taxable income from unpaid productive effort, our data base on the subject is considerably less than adequate. There are measurement problems in evaluating unpaid productive effort that are far more serious than those

---

James N. Morgan is a research scientist at the Institute for Social Research, and professor of economics at the University of Michigan.

found in assessing paid work, which at least has some readily available data in the form of wages. Particularly after taxes, wages may not measure productivity precisely, but they are commonly accepted as an approximation, assuming that markets, even for labor, work reasonably well and that taxes are not too unfair or discrepant.

But how should we value unpaid work? For those who also work for wages we could argue that they rationally equate their marginal returns in the two kinds of activity, but there are difficulties with this approach. Many people, particularly among the young who do the most unpaid work, claim to want more work than they can find; others get higher overtime wages than their regular wage. Also, imputing wages to those not currently working poses serious problems of "selection bias" for which there are only proximate solutions. And many unpaid productive activities have a component of pleasure, or direct consumption. Parents may well spend more time caring for their children than just what is required for investment in their education and rearing (human capital), and many a home gardener does things that he or she would not pay others to do.*

Others have proposed valuing unpaid productive time according to market wages paid for that kind of activity, even breaking down such activities as housework and child care into components for the purpose. This method, however, requires very detailed accounts of activities, complete with time-diaries, and so far has not proved practical for large-scale research.

Given these circumstances, and particularly the lack of much variation in the reports of amounts saved per hour in relation to paid earnings, this paper focuses on hours devoted to productive activities, which are defined here as activities that produce goods or services that otherwise would have to be paid for. This paper looks at hours reported as spent per year in such activities without attempting to solve the problem of potentially different values depending on who is putting in the hours or what the activity is. For example, for work done on the car or house, in which case

---

* We have, in the case of do-it-yourself activities, asked people how much they think they saved by doing that activity. After subtracting the cost of materials and the recreational aspects, we tended to get amounts that appear reasonable—in relation to the hours reported spent—implying modest hourly earnings. Those implied earnings do not vary much with the individual's paid wage, however.

we asked about both hours and the amount of money saved, both can be reported. In the case of growing and preserving food, we asked only about amounts saved, on the assumption that people could not recall the scattered hours spent on these activities.

Among the data presented here on hours spent in various unpaid productive activities are the following: For some activities difficult to attribute to individuals, there are data at the family level: volunteer work for organizations (for example, churches and charities), time helping friends and other individuals, and repairing houses or cars. At the individual level there are data on housework, in relation to paid market employment, and on time kept available for paid work but diverted by unemployment, strikes, illness, or caring for others who are ill. Here we follow men and women separately, focusing on age differences and only occasionally going beyond age to the demographic changes that affect the use of people's time: marriage, children, home ownership, and length of residence in an area.

Most of the data are from a pair of national studies on philanthropy that were conducted for the Commission on Private Philanthropy and Public Needs (Morgan et al., 1979). Although there are a few other studies on volunteer activity and, of course, many larger samples giving data on paid work hours, this paper deals primarily with data from the two studies referred to. There are also time-budget studies in progress at the Institute of Social Research (ISR) that report time use over a whole year or for an average week (Hill, forthcoming). Preliminary comparisons indicate no glaring discrepancies.

In comparing individuals or families, a researcher must either use the same short period, expand to a uniform longer period, or use the longer period in the questions. The presumed accuracy of time-diary reports on yesterday is substantially reduced when they must be multiplied by 365, but—a more important issue—interpersonal comparisons can be distorted. Because diaries compel accounting for 24 hours, however, they can be useful in perhaps constraining the exaggerations one might get in asking about only one or two activities. We must assume that by asking about all of last year, we may get exaggeration from a respondent's focusing on a few things, which is offset by understatement from memory loss. In the case of housework and child care where we ask about current time per week, we may also get some exaggeration, compounded by the fact that people can do more than one thing at a time.

PRODUCTIVE ACTIVITIES MEASURED AT THE FAMILY LEVEL

Volunteer Time

In 1974 we interviewed two national samples: one based on an area probability sample and the other on an Internal Revenue Service sample interviewed by the Census Bureau that asked about gifts of time and money to organizations and to individuals (Morgan et al., 1979).

The pooled data indicated that some 6 billion hours a year were given to religious and charitable organizations in 1973, somewhat more than half of it by husbands and single (male and female) heads of households. If this time were valued at some reasonable opportunity-cost wage, it would be roughly equivalent to the aggregate money contributions that year. And even though it is mostly education that accounts for differences in volunteer time and income that accounts for differences in the donation of money, the two forms of altruism go together: Those who gave time also gave money. Clearly, then, there is a philanthropy syndrome. We know much less, however, about the dynamics by which people begin either type of philanthropy (donating time or money), or whether there is some order in which they get into the syndrome. The few questions we asked about parents' altruism had little explanatory power.

It was mostly the well-educated, the affluent, and the young who gave time to church or charity, and even among these groups a few gave substantial amounts while many gave little or none, making the aggregate estimates shaky. There was also time spent helping friends, neighbors, or relatives (for example, caring for sick persons not living with the individual surveyed). Some 30 percent of families reported giving some such time, again with a few giving a lot, and a crude estimate of the aggregate for 1973 was 2 billion hours, as compared to the 6 billion hours donated to organizations.

The focus in this paper is on age, particularly in view of the changing age distribution of the population. But because volunteer time is so strongly affected by education, and education is correlated with age, we can see a purer age relationship by relating each individual's volunteer time to the average for his or her education group (averaging the ratio of husbands and wives for families containing married couples). Table 1 shows that there is

TABLE 1 Time Given to Philanthropic Organizations, in 1973, in Hours and in Relation to the Average for One's Education Group

Age	Average Hours per Household	Ratio of Time to Average for Each Individual's Education Group
18–34	58	0.58
35–44	132	1.09
45–54	91	0.84
55–64	94	0.84
65–74	63	0.80
75+	60	0.72

still an age pattern although it is somewhat attenuated. The greatest time in relation to the amount expected for one's education level is given at the very age when the combination of job and family is putting the most pressure on people's time anyway. When looking at age differences, however, one must always speculate whether they also or merely reflect cohort differences among the generations. There could be a pure decline with age plus a tendency for the younger generation to be less altruistic, and of course there are more one-person households at both ends of the age spectrum.

We also know from an earlier study asking about all volunteer work—for organizations *or* relatives—that income dominated the explanations, so much so that, surprisingly, the single best predictor was the number of modern appliances in the home (Morgan et al., 1966). But the next best predictor was education, followed by long residence in an area. Age never accounted for much in that analysis. In some earlier studies of retirement we asked people not yet retired whether they expected to do more volunteer work when they retired, and we asked the retired whether they were doing more volunteer work than before retirement. Of course these are different generations or cohorts and there are undoubtedly memory biases, but substantially more expected to increase their volunteer work than reported having done so (Barfield and Morgan, 1969).

A major implication of these findings is that it is not available time that seems to drive philanthropic activity but abilities and purposes. People with children get involved in activities, ranging from church to Little League, that are directed at the socialization of their offspring. Active, visible people are urged to take leadership roles, and the more money they give, the more they are asked also to give time. All this is indirect inference, however, as I know of no studies of the dynamic process. Tax laws would appear to encourage more time donations, in comparison to money donations, among low-income people who do not itemize and cannot therefore get income tax rebates on their charitable contributions of money. But they may also be spending more time earning a living or looking for more paid work.

The other implications of the data are that paid work and unpaid work do not appear to be interchangeable and that the reduction in paid work hours with age, even after retirement, does not appear to lead to any substantial increase in volunteer work. Perhaps incentives are more important than free time. With volunteer work we usually assume that the opportunities are there.

Emergency Help

From many studies we know that there is relatively little money being given to relatives not living together and not much time regularly devoted to such things as caring for grandchildren. A recent analysis of a sample close to retirement age found only 1 in 40 persons currently providing any support for parents (L. Morgan, 1983). But a major element in interfamily help might be the availability of help in emergencies. The 1980 interviews of the Panel Study of Income Dynamics asked about emergency giving or receiving of time or money to or from friends or relatives in the previous five years. A chapter in Volume 10 of *Five Thousand American Families* gives the details of the findings (Morgan, 1983). A summary will have to suffice here.

In the study we asked about whether emergency help was given and to whom or from whom; we also asked about availability and, in the case of money, whether it was to be repaid and if so whether it would be repaid with interest. The focus was on time rather than money, but from the data it can be said that the giving of money in emergencies was largely from those in their peak earning years to their children. Four out of five persons felt some emergency help would be available to them in an emergency, and two out of three said money help was available. But what about *actual* time help?

A constant 30 percent of the individuals surveyed reported

giving some time in the past five years, at all ages until the most advanced. After 75 the frequency dropped off. A smaller fraction reported getting help, indicating some memory bias but perhaps also a tendency for those in trouble to get help from more than one person. Reports of getting time help fell with age from an early 20 percent to a little over 10 percent of those aged 55 to 64; the figure then rose to slightly over 20 percent for those aged 75 and older.

Admittedly these are crude data, based on fuzzy recall and a somewhat ambiguous definition of giving, but they indicate relatively little activity. On the other hand, the vast majority indicated help would be available, and this insurance aspect may be more important than the actual time spent.

Unpaid Productive Work Around the House

The remaining activity that has been measured mostly at the family or household level is home production or do-it-yourself activities: repairing or improving homes or cars, or growing or preserving food. Prior to the Panel Study, similar questions were asked in the 1965 *Productive Americans* study (Morgan et al., 1966). They covered the year 1964, asking separately and specifically about the following:

Percentage Yes
- 100 Work around the house, such as preparing meals, cleaning, and straightening up
- 50 Painting, redecorating, or major housecleaning
- 78 Sewing or mending (women only)
- 25 Growing own food
- 24 Canning or freezing
- 25 Anything else that saved you from having to hire someone else to do it
- 46 Volunteer work without pay such as work for church or charity or helping relatives
- 17 Taking courses or lessons (investing in self) (head of family only)

The other side of the coin was also considered, namely, whether the family paid to have outside help with these activities:

Percentage Yes
- 14 Things that have to be done around the house, such as preparing meals, cleaning, and making repairs
- 30 Sending out any of the laundry

10 Care of children
80 Eating out (42 percent over a week or more)
14 Painting, redecorating, or spring cleaning
16 Lawn work

Although substantial fractions of respondents reported buying back some of their own time in these ways, the amounts reported were usually trivially small.

When we totaled the five items of home production in the first list above, they came to a total of 205 hours per year (heads and wives together). It was discovered that it was not age that mattered but the absence of one or more inhibiting factors, many associated with the family life course. Those who did the most such work were married, lived in single-family structures with large families, had a highly educated family head, lived in a rural area, and had no young children under two years of age. (A systematic search program resulted in such a high-order interaction.) When the residuals from that analysis were examined in a second search, which included some potentially endogenous variables like home ownership, only home ownership and a measure of achievement motivation mattered.

Because the crude separate quantification by brackets makes quantitative analysis difficult, and because we have more recent data on home production, we turn to the Panel Study of Income Dynamics, which in 1968 to 1972 and in 1979 asked about these activities in the previous year: (1) hours spent repairing cars, (2) money saved repairing cars, (3) hours spent working on the house, (4) money saved working on the house, and (5) money saved growing or preserving food.

Sewing or mending had been part of the ways people said they saved on clothing costs in 1968, but those questions were dropped because few people reported saving more than $200 on clothes in any way. We also asked in 1968 to 1972 whether the respondent was taking any courses or lessons—a steady 11 to 12 percent said yes each year.

The proportions of individuals that reported working on cars or houses were remarkably stable—a little over a third of the households each year—except for a substantial increase in reported work on the house for 1971 in relation to the four years before or the report seven years later.

Because more recent years have seen increases in both unemployment and inflation to pressure people toward more productive use of their time, we compare 1972 with 1979 estimates of such activities in 1971 and 1978. Table 2 shows modest increases in the proportions that report working on their car or growing food, and a decrease, perhaps toward normalcy, in reports of working on the house. For those who like to compare cohorts we give the 1978 estimates both by age in early 1979 and by age in early 1972. More important, the table shows that it is largely the young who work on cars, the middle-aged who work on their homes, and the older people who grow food.

The age patterns are similar when we ask for the average amounts saved in the three activities (Table 3), although the effect is partly automatic because the averages include the zeroes of those who reported no activity. Note, however, that the average amount saved by working on the house increased substantially while the proportion reporting any fell, implying fewer but larger projects.

For work on cars and on the house we asked both hours and amounts saved so that we could estimate the implied hourly earnings from the activities. Table 4 shows it by age, with people aged 24 to 45 apparently doing things that required more skill, or valuing their time more highly. Marginalists will notice that this is not the marginal wage on do-it-yourself activities but the average; it does not allow us to model decisions about unpaid versus paid work, even after adjusting for income taxes on the latter. Indeed, if we look at the implied earnings per hour working on cars or houses according to the hourly earnings of the respondent, there is almost no correlation.

Unpaid do-it-yourself work was also affected by marital status, whether the wife worked for money, home ownership, and the gender of single household heads. There was no apparent substitution of time—no negative correlation between paid work and unpaid work. (Indeed, there was a positive correlation that disappeared when we took account of age, sex, marital status, a working wife, and home ownership.) Nor was there any apparent marginal comparison of earnings. There was, in fact a *positive* simple correlation between paid wage rates and hours of unpaid work, which again withered in the multivariate analysis. Those not in the labor force at all did less unpaid work, too, perhaps the extra free time being more than offset by a lack of opportunities or skills, or by disabilities.

TABLE 2 Percentage Who Saved *Any* Money Working on Car or House or Growing Food, by Age and Age Cohorts

	Car			House			Food		
	1971[a]	1978[a]		1971[a]	1978[a]		1971[a]	1978[a]	
	1972 Age	1979 Age	1972 Age	1972 Age	1979 Age	1972 Age	1972 Age	1979 Age	1972 Age
Age									
18–24	45%	51%	55%	21%	25%	29%	11%	16%	19%
25–34	50	58	57	49	44	48	27	25	28
35–44	43	54	51	55	46	45	31	35	34
45–54	30	45	42	53	45	42	31	38	39
55–64	26	33	29	37	34	32	32	41	43
65–74	13	18	13	33	23	20	38	40	37
75+	4	6	5	15	9	6	32	32	32
All ages	35	42	42	43	35	35	29	32	32

[a]Year for which activities are estimated.

TABLE 3 Dollars Saved With Do-It-Yourself Work, by Age Group and Age Cohorts (for 5,080 families in 1972 and 6,373 families in 1979)

	Car			House			Food		
	1971[a,b]	1978[b]		1971[a,b]	1978[b]		1971[a,b]	1978[b]	
Age	1972 Age	1979 Age	1972 Age	1972 Age	1979 Age	1972 Age	1972 Age	1979 Age	1972 Age
18–24	$104	$163	$185	$127	$194	$297	$15	$22	$ 25
25–34	96	176	154	352	502	535	34	45	58
35–44	88	137	151	390	531	478	61	77	91
45–54	79	141	113	304	349	348	58	80	63
55–64	42	73	60	162	252	182	62	89	102
65–74	14	27	15	143	112	99	50	59	52
75+	3	5	3	36	43	11	34	69	69
All ages	69	118	118	252	327	327	47	62	62

[a]In 1978 dollars.
[b]Year for which activities are estimated.

TABLE 4 1978 Implied Hourly Earnings From Do-It-Yourself Savings, by Age

Age in 1979	Cars			House			Number of Cases
	$	Hours	$/Hour	$	Hours	$/Hour	
18–24	163	21.8	7.48	194	27.8	6.98	947
25–34	176	18.1	9.72	502	41.9	11.98	1,995
35–44	138	14.5	9.52	531	42.1	12.61	928
45–54	142	19.2	7.40	349	31.6	9.54	923
55–64	73	8.5	8.59	252	37.6	6.70	770
65–74	27	5.3	5.09	112	11.9	9.41	539
75+	5	1.0	5.00	43	7.8	5.51	271
All ages	118	13.9	8.49	327	32.4	10.09	6,373

Most important of all for our discussion here, these unpaid productive activities drop off with advanced age, in spite of more free time, lower incomes, and greater home ownership. It seems unlikely that this is a cohort effect and that today's young will continue their work activities unabated, although they might be healthier and affected by their unemployment and inflation experiences. We have no information about their accumulation of human capital (skills), an accumulation that might presage more such activity by them than by earlier generations. Indeed, without question there is a need to collect such information.

PRODUCTIVE ACTIVITIES MEASURED AT THE INDIVIDUAL LEVEL

Housework

Housework hours for regular cooking, cleaning, and the like are clearly dominated by family composition and, among families with two adults and not more than one child, by the wife's absorption in paid work. Indeed, relatively few subgroups account for 41 percent of the variance in housework hours. Figure 1 shows the subgroups that do this, though we must remember that a search program found them in a sequential process examining many alternatives at each step; tests and extrapolations thus are suspect. Many other analyses indicate that when a wife goes to work, her leisure suffers more than her housework and her husband is unlikely to increase his work contribution around the house appreciably.

Simple descriptions of the hours spent in productive activity by gender and age fail to illuminate the forces associated with gender and age that really affect productive effort. A considerable amount of work in labor economics attempts to fit utility maximizing models of choices between market and nonmarket work and between work and leisure. But this work is hampered by the fact that none of our surveys has provided these researchers with information on people's alternative opportunities nor on their marginal wage rates. There is a kind of natural experiment, however, in the changing composition of families if we are willing to treat these changes as approximately exogenous in the short run. People do make decisions about who lives with whom

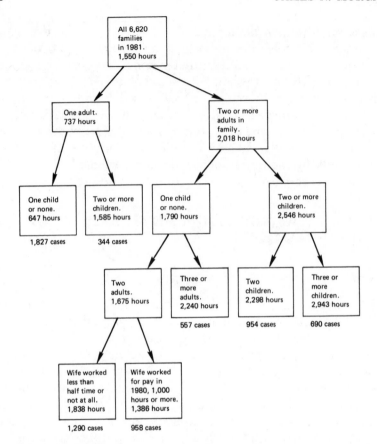

FIGURE 1   The housework hours of families as determined during interviews conducted in 1981.

and about having children and about when the children leave home; but individuals inevitably grow one year older each year and many other family changes are in large part determined by social and legal forces.

Table 5 relates the level of or changes in total housework of the family to the number of individuals, or changes in that number, by age and gender (Morgan, forthcoming). In spite of the rather crude method of measuring housework and the fact that differences are subject to large relative errors, all the regression coefficients for family composition are highly significant and intuitively sensible. A baby adds greatly to housework, teenaged sons

TABLE 5 Level or Change in Housework Hours As Affected by Level or Change in Number of Family Members or Wife's Paid Work

Level or Change in	Level 1979	Change 1975–1980	1978–1980	Level 1979	Change 1975–1980	1978–1980
Number of:						
Children aged 0–2	357	337	374	345	336	364
Children aged 3–5	222	174	204	218	174	243
Children aged 6–13	314	248	345	325	247	343
Daughters aged 14–17	396	282	347	418	283	345
Sons aged 14–17	319	262	230	340	262	230
Daughters aged 18–20	297	288	326	306	281	335
Sons aged 18–20	126	194	220	148	194	220
Daughters aged 21–29	169	261	355	163	261	359
Sons aged 21–29	272	174	190	285	173	190
Others	797	455	568	898	458	597
Wife's paid work				−.21	(−.03)[a]	−.10

[a] ( ) = Not significant.

add less than teenaged daughters, and other adults add most of all. Since we have some families that add or lose a spouse, much of the change in "others" is marriage or divorce.

If we include the change in the wife's paid work hours as a pseudoexplanatory variable, dodging the simultaneity of decisions about paid work and housework, there would appear to be a small short-run dynamic effect. There is no significant effect for longer lags, but a large significant cross-section or long-term effect does occur, which may well reflect interpersonal differences in preferences or skills rather than individual marginal choices.

The effects of a change in family composition on the wife's paid work is much less clear. There are practically no dynamic effects in this case except for changes in "others," which is partially an artifact of the circumstance that an increase or decrease in "others" often means a spouse and without a spouse there cannot be a wife to work for money. A change in the housework hours has no effect on the wife's paid work hours in the dynamic data, leaving the suspicion that the static negative correlation between housework and the wife's paid work hours is spurious, resulting from omitted variables.

We will turn now to some other data on individuals. In our examination we will identify their own hours of productive work, again focusing on age-gender patterns without going much beyond marital status, and investigate other variables such as home ownership, job seniority, or family size, which might be affecting the results.

Lifetime Patterns of Family Situations for Individuals

The activities of individuals over their life course are affected by their family situations, particularly whether they live with a spouse and whether there are children under 18 at home. For the 1981 wave of the Panel Study sample individuals, Table 6 shows their distribution within each age group according to family situation. One can estimate the probability for a man or woman of being a household head or wife, and then the probability of living with a spouse, followed by the probability of having children at home. The probability of being neither household head (householder) nor wife is of course 100 percent for young children, remains appreciable for the late teens and early twenties, and then only rises again for those 75 or older.

TABLE 6 Gender and Family Status by Age in 1981 for 15,797 Sample Individuals (percentage)

	0–17	18–24	25–34	35–44	45–54	55–61	62–64	65–69	70–74	75+	Ages
Male heads											
Men without wives	0	14	27	24	20	27	31	33	35	39	17
No children	0	10	13	7	10	22	27	31	35	38	11
Children	0	4	14	17	10	5	4	2	0	1	6
Married men	0	4	17	22	24	19	11	6	3	1	10
No children	0	3	5	3	12	15	10	5	3	1	4
Children	0	1	12	19	12	4	1	1	0	0	6
Female heads	0	12	14	10	13	17	21	25	33	41	12
No children	0	8	7	3	8	15	19	24	32	40	9
Children	0	4	7	7	5	2	2	1	1	1	3
Wives	0	15	34	42	41	35	36	33	27	12	22
No children	0	6	6	6	24	31	34	32	26	12	10
Children	0	9	28	36	17	4	2	1	1	0	12
Others (both genders)	100	56	7	2	2	2	2	2	2	7	38
Total (percent)	100	101	99	100	100	100	101	99	100	100	99
Number of cases	5,970	2,414	2,583	1,337	1,370	799	298	431	320	375	15,797

There are more precise demographic data from the U.S. Census Bureau, but we present these partly to reassure the reader that the Panel Study sample still reasonably represents the country as a whole. The patterns move smoothly through the life course. Multivariate analyses of housework hours, for example, would take account of family status, age and numbers of children, and age that is a proxy for several of these situational variables. On the other hand, the resulting patterns are strong and systematic by age without getting into the process details.

Housework

The major unpaid productive activity in most households is housework, which is usually combined with child care. Only in one year of the Panel Study (1976) when we interviewed the wives, too, did we ask separately about child care. It is useful to compare husbands' reports from other years on housework done by their wives and themselves with the 1976 reports by wives on their housework and child care and their husbands' child care. (Even in that year husbands were asked about their own housework time.)*

Analysis of the effects of family composition on *total family* housework hours revealed systematic and meaningful effects of individuals by age and gender, whether estimated from a single cross-section or by using the panel to relate changes in family composition to changes in housework.

Table 7 shows the age patterns of housework–child care hours of individuals by gender, containing some of these family-composition effects. Table 8 uses the 1976 interviews in which the wife reported on the husband's child care, but he reported his own housework, perhaps with some duplication. Adding child care explicitly increases the estimates of unpaid work for married men and women.

---

*Note that housework was elicited by three questions asked of the husband, or two (the second and third) asked of single heads: (1) About how much time does your wife spend on housework in an average week? I mean time spent cooking, cleaning, and doing other work around the house. (2) About how much time do *you* (head) spend on housework in an average week? I mean time spent cooking, cleaning, and doing other work around the house. (3) Does anyone else here in the household help with the housework? This final question was asked of each respondent: About how much time does he/she spend on housework in an average week?

TABLE 7 Annual Housework Hours by Age, Gender, and Marital Status, From 1981 Interviews About Parental Status

Age in 1980	Men				Women				
		Married			Single		Married[a]		
	Single	All	With Children	All Men	All	With Children	All	With Children	All Women
≤24	429	364	330	396	704	1,081	1,225	1,492	988
25–34	425	375	375	386	741	1,050	1,452	1,584	1,240
35–44	349	300	300	308	877	969	1,532	1,617	1,399
45–54	476	365	344	374	962	1,296	1,435	1,565	1,320
55–61	588	376	454	401	974	1,116	1,462	1,972	1,306
62–64	(771)[b]	530	(526)	549	960	(827)	1,534	(1,723)	1,321
65–69	(722)	505	(297)	534	863	(1,097)	1,482	(1,239)	1,216
70–74	(891)	478	(169)	575	974	(1,263)	1,519	(404)	1,220
75+	690	493	(716)	565	842	(1,075)	1,279	—	944
All ages	491	384	350	407	848	1,076	1,448	1,587	1,237
N	884	2,592	1,538	3,476	1,950	832	2,710	1,612	4,660

[a]Wives' hours are reported by their husbands.
[b]( ) = Fewer than 25 cases.

TABLE 8   Annual Hours of Housework Plus Child Care, From 1976 Interviews

Age in 1976	Housework					
	Men			Women		
	Single	Married	All	Single	Married[a]	All
18–24	426	624	554	385	2,111	1,532
25–34	377	761	695	527	2,461	2,045
35–44	446	690	668	805	2,059	1,807
45–54	558	427	436	862	1,620	1,462
55–61	677	282	308	898	1,426	1,244
62–64	471	398	405	899	1,168	1,066
65–69	891	350	406	829	1,194	1,018
70–74	709	471	501	962	1,062	109
75+	690	462	534	893	882	891
Averages	484	559	548	741	1,899	1,549

[a]Wives reported for themselves. Questions referred to hours per week at the time of the interview.

Total Productive Use of Time

We can define productive use of time (or offer of time) as including:

- paid employment or self-employment;
- commuting time;
- strike or unemployment time;
- time lost from work by illness of self or others;
- housework and child care (including time given in return for child care);
- volunteer work for organizations (church, charity)
- time spent helping friends and relatives;
- unpaid productive work on house, car, food, and clothing (sewing); and
- taking courses or lessons (investment in human capital).

In addition, if people report that they wanted more (or less) work than they could get last year, we might infer that their "supply" of labor was actually greater. (If they were currently unemployed, we did not ask the question, but in this analysis we treat these people as though the answer was yes.) The question was only asked of heads of households, not wives, except in 1976.

Substitutions of Paid and Unpaid Productive Time

Economic models focus on marginal choices, leading to the notion that when paid market work becomes less available, unpaid productive activities might flourish. The response to economic incentives at the margin, however, may well be overwhelmed by constraints and pressures. And we have already seen that volunteer work is largely done by young overworked people with children and that most older people do not report doing more volunteer work after they retired. Housework hours reported do tend to rise a little, particularly for men in their 60s.

Hence we look at housework, paid work, and the total supply of productive hours, in which we include commuting time and hours lost from work because of strikes, unemployment, or illness of self or others. From the individual's point of view that total is what it takes to earn his standard of living, even though society may only see the benefit of the hours that are paid for plus the housework.

The 1981 reports on housework currently available, and reports on the other work times for the prior year, show the expected patterns, with the fraction of the total hours that are paid for declining after age 40 for men and from the beginning for women (Table 9). Particularly for women, of course, there may well be a historic trend or generation effect added to the age effect as succeeding generations of women have fewer children and work more for money even when there are children at home.

Because married women's hours are reported by their husbands in most years of the Panel, we also provide some estimates from the 1976 interviews in which wives were also interviewed and separate questions were asked about child care. Here there may still be some bias in favor of husbands, who reported their own housework, perhaps double-counting some of the time their wives credited them for as doing child care. The patterns, however, are much the same (Table 10).

Individual Change

Admittedly, we have been using the Panel Study of Income Dynamics in an inefficient way—as a series of cross-sections providing different information in different years. Life course

TABLE 9 Hours of Work[a] in 1981, by Age and Gender

	Men				Women			
Age in 1981	Paid Work	Housework	Total Supply	Percentage of Total Paid	Paid Work	Housework	Total Supply	Percentage of Total Paid
18–24	1,919	396	2,710	71	1,122	988	2,332	48
25–34	2,094	386	2,825	74	1,150	1,240	2,606	44
35–44	2,250	308	2,841	79	1,142	1,399	2,694	42
45–54	2,048	374	2,702	76	1,068	1,320	2,541	42
55–61	1,754	401	2,421	72	790	1,306	2,206	36
62–64	1,170	549	1,854	63	354	1,321	1,754	20
65–69	473	534	1,036	46	248	1,216	1,490	17
70–74	433	675	1,057	41	149	1,220	1,440	11
75+	142	565	726	20	20	944	969	1
All Ages	1,747	407	2,417	72	876	1,237	2,257	39
N			3,476				4,660	

[a]Includes paid hours, housework, and time lost from paid work because of unemployment, strikes, or illness of self or others. Wives' hours are reported by their husbands.

TABLE 10 Paid Work Hours and Total Supplied Work Hours, by Age, Gender, and Marital Status for 1975[a]

| | Men | | | | | | Women | | | | | |
| | Single | | | Married | | | Single | | | Married | | |
Age in 1976	Paid Hours	Total Hours Supplied	Percentage Paid	Paid Hours	Total Hours Supplied	Percentage Paid	Paid Hours	Total Hours Supplied	Percentage Paid	Paid Hours	Total Hours Supplied	Percentage Paid
18–24	2,036	2,462	83	2,376	3,000	79	785	1,170	67	1,238	3,349	37
25–34	2,340	2,717	86	2,530	3,291	77	1,091	1,618	67	1,193	3,654	33
35–44	2,375	2,821	84	2,581	3,271	79	1,245	2,050	61	1,123	3,182	35
45–54	2,110	2,668	79	2,401	2,828	85	1,445	2,307	63	1,042	2,662	34
55–61	1,679	2,356	71	2,115	2,398	88	1,220	2,118	58	838	2,264	37
62–64	(1,356)[b]	(1,827)	(74)	1,613	2,011	80	803	1,692	49	416	1,584	26
65–69	(120)	(1,011)	(12)	946	1,296	73	468	1,297	36	289	1,483	19
70–74	(365)	(1,074)	(34)	304	775	39	191	1,453	17	89	1,151	8
75+	(25)	(715)	(35)	295	757	39	78	971	8	(14)	(896)	(2)
All ages	1,853	2,337	79	2,177	2,736	80	866	1,607	54	1,003	2,902	35

[a]Wives' interviews for their work supply and husband's child care, husbands' reports on their housework, paid work, and work supply. "Supply" includes the hours unemployed, on strike, lost from work by illness of self or others, and commuting.

[b]( ) = Fewer than 25 cases.

changes of individuals can in fact be studied and analyzed more carefully. One can even pool these changes—for example, by creating a record for each person for each three-year period he or she was in the Panel and was either a household head or wife. Taking such a file we produced 66,326 records, but because we omitted the questions on housework in one year, three years worth of triplets must be discarded in looking at housework, which leaves 42,500 records. Table 11 shows the average changes for men and women in their paid work and housework, and for comparison the average level of hours for the year between the two measuring the change. It is clear that paid work increases for only a few years, then falls off at an increasing rate, which is dramatized by our selection of age ranges. Housework, on the other hand,

TABLE 11 Mean Two-Year Change in Paid Hours and in Housework, by Age and Gender, Compared With Mid-Year Levels (for 42,500 Records of Sample Household Heads or Wives for Each Available Three-Year Period)

Age in Mid-Year	Paid Hours		Housework	
	Middle-Year Level	Change From Year 1 to Year 3	Middle-Year Level	Change From Year 1 to Year 3
Men				
18–29	2,135	102	863	42
30–39	2,309	5	1,023	−36
40–49	2,223	−25	1,109	−50
50–54	2,058	−72	923	−48
55–59	1,925	−123	858	−21
60–61	1,677	−277	884	33
62	1,557	−342	904	28
63–64	1,350	−566	999	−85
65	792	−625	928	46
66+	412	−105	864	−47
Women				
18–29	970	25	1,389	52
30–39	847	66	1,593	−75
40–49	914	48	1,506	−81
50–54	897	−3	1,398	97
55–59	837	−64	1,291	−11
60–61	745	−160	1,251	−43
62	583	−203	1,330	−70
63–64	454	−188	1,305	17
65	246	−217	1,320	−86
66+	130	−48	1,251	−74

declines much less sharply and even seems to increase a little around retirement age. It is likely that reports on housework hours are considerably less accurate than the reports on paid work hours because the husband is reporting paid hours and housework hours for both spouses in families containing a married couple.

The mean changes appear to reflect the changes in the means, of course. It is when one wants to study interpersonal differences in these patterns that the Panel data become advantageous. Our earlier analysis of the effects of change in family composition on housework is an example.

Expressed Desires for More or Less Work

One reason for looking at the total supply of hours is that a person may have to devote more hours to earning a living than he or she is paid for–that is, the total supply includes unpaid commuting, strike, and sick time. But beyond that there is an additional labor supply we can only call underemployment. We attempt to tap it by asking people whether they could have worked more (or less) last year and if not whether they would have liked more (or less) work. Tables 12 and 13 show a very few at any age reporting wanting less work, even at less pay. More importantly, the tables show substantial proportions, particularly among the young, saying they wanted more work than was available. We went back to 1976 because wives were asked about their own desires then, whereas for the 1981 interviews we can only report on husbands and on single male and female household heads. One serendipitous finding is the appearance of a substantial increase between 1976 and 1981 in the proportion of young single women aged 18 to 44 who said they wanted more work. There was a smaller increase among the younger single men. Of course, there was also an increase in unemployment, which hit the young the hardest. Although the question was not asked of the currently unemployed, we assume that they wanted more work.

There is a pervasive myth that many people who would rather keep on working are forced to retire, in spite of a variety of studies over many years that show most people retire from paid work as soon as they can afford to, and rarely regret it (Streib, 1971; Parnes, 1970; Morgan, 1980). The elimination of compul-

TABLE 12 Reports of Having Wanted More Paid Work, or Less Work Even at Less Pay, During 1975[a]

Age in 1976	Wanted More Work				Wanted Less Work			
	Men		Women		Men		Women	
	Single	Married	Single	Married	Single	Married	Single	Married
18–24	39.1	43.3	17.4	16.0	3.1	3.1	1.6	2.5
25–34	18.1	24.9	16.5	13.4	4.7	3.2	1.6	4.8
35–44	21.7	25.2	15.7	11.8	0.0	3.1	5.4	4.2
45–54	24.0	19.2	25.3	11.5	6.9	2.7	0.0	3.9
55–61	19.2	14.5	10.0	2.9	0.7	3.2	3.2	3.5
62–64	(0)[b]	7.9	6.0	0.1	(14.6)	1.4	2.1	1.6
65–69	(0)	0.1	3.5	3.1	(0)	1.3	0.1	0.0
70–74	(0)	0.0	2.1	0.0	(0)	0.0	0.0	0.0
75+	(0)	3.5	1.2	(0.0)	(0)	0.0	0.0	(0.0)
All ages	21.9	20.7	12.3	10.5	3.3	2.7	1.6	3.5
N	499	2,350	1,429	2,480				

[a]In the 1976 reports, wives reported for themselves what they had wanted during 1975. Those not in the labor force were not asked. The unemployed were assumed to want more work.

[b]( ) = Fewer than 25 cases.

TABLE 13 Desire for Less or More Work in 1980^a (1981 Interviews)

Age	Men No Wife Less	Men No Wife More	Married Less	Married More	All Men Less	All Men More	Women Heads Less	Women Heads More
18–24	3.9	45.9	1.8	36.3	3.4	43.6	2.3	37.8
25–34	4.7	30.1	4.5	25.2	4.6	28.2	7.2	26.0
35–44	4.8	25.1	1.6	22.9	3.2	24.0	3.8	21.1
45–54	2.8	27.1	5.3	17.6	4.2	21.8	5.9	19.1
55–61	5.9	12.9	4.6	17.2	5.4	14.6	4.0	6.9
62–64	3.0	4.7	4.5	4.0	3.4	4.5	0.0	8.8
65–69	1.9	1.0	4.9	0.6	2.4	0.9	0.0	2.6
70–74	3.1	0	0	15.4	2.9	1.1	1.1	1.1
75+	0	0	0	0	0	0	0	0.7
All ages		32.2		21.2		21.1		16.2
Number of cases	2,232		1,244		3,476		1,950	

^{a}The currently unemployed are assumed to have wanted more work.

TABLE 14 Percentage of People With Some Disability Limiting the Type or Amount of Work the Person Can Do, by Age, Gender, and Marital Status (1981 Interviews for All Husbands, Wives, and Single Household Heads)

Age	Men			Women		
	Single	Married	All Men	Single	Married[a]	All Women
18–24	9.8	7.4	8.5	4.4	8.1	6.4
25–34	8.2	6.0	6.6	8.2	3.9	5.2
35–44	16.0	9.2	10.3	13.8	10.2	10.9
45–54	26.5	18.8	14.8	32.7	11.9	17.0
55–61	33.5	29.1	29.5	42.6	27.0	32.0
62–64	(45.6)[b]	33.4	34.3	48.2	30.8	37.3
65–69	(48.5)	40.0	41.9	52.0	36.2	43.0
70–74	67.4	38.9	45.6	59.5	41.7	51.4
75+	61.3	60.5	60.8	59.9	45.8	56.6
All ages	22.6	18.1	19.1	31.4	14.6	20.5
Number of cases	844	2,592	3,476	1,950	2,710	4,660

[a] Wives' disabilities are by husbands' reports.
[b] ( ) = Fewer than 25 cases.

sory retirement, even when combined with inflationary pressures, appears to have had little effect on when people retire, although providing more flexible hours and appropriate working conditions might produce some changes.

Capacity—Illness and Disability

It is commonly agreed that not only are people living longer—their health also is better. Substantial changes do occur with aging, however. Using the Panel Study data, I include two tables on illness and disability (even though there are much better data on health and disability). Table 14 shows the percentage of people, by age and gender and marital status, who report disabilities that limit the type or amount of work they can do (as before, husbands report for their wives as well). The dramatic increase in this measure with age raises questions about the productive potential of an older population if no attention is paid to these physical limitations. The much higher reported incidence of disability among unmarried (single, widowed, divorced, or separated) people says nothing about causal direction and may be partly the result of a reporting bias (more time to focus on one's own problems). The higher incidence may also be explained—at least for women—by the direct reports made by single women as compared to the husbands' reports for wives. The apparent tendency for more women than men to be disabled in the middle years may also reflect that, with more husbands reporting for both, men may understate their own disabilities in relation to those of their wives. It is the general age pattern that concerns us here.

Table 15 shows the expected increase in disability and hospitalization with age but a flatter pattern of intensive illness (sick bed days).

Some Traps in Comparing Age Groups

We have all become familiar with the age-period-cohort paradox: We are aware that what seems to be an effect of age can be a difference between generations and that a change in the same people over time can be the effects of a historic period (changing levels of inflation and unemployment) rather than an effect of growing older. But there are other problems.

TABLE 15 Self-Reports on Limits to Work, Days Sick in Bed, and Nights in Hospitals in 1980

Age	Men				Women			
	Percent Disabled	Sick Bed Days	Hospital Nights	Number of Cases	Percent Disabled	Sick Bed Days	Hospital Nights	Number of Cases
18–24	8.5	2.9	0.8	384	6.4	3.6	1.2	624
25–34	6.6	2.4	0.6	1,079	5.2	2.9	1.2	1,243
35–44	10.3	2.3	0.7	552	10.9	2.7	0.9	747
45–54	14.8	2.4	1.4	553	17.0	3.7	1.5	793
55–61	29.5	5.3	2.7	348	32.0	4.7	1.7	438
62–64	34.3	3.0	2.3	127	37.3	4.0	2.9	168
65–69	41.9	2.9	2.7	170	43.0	6.6	3.4	251
70–74	45.6	3.6	3.6	117	51.4	6.9	2.7	197
75+	60.8	4.3	4.9	146	56.6	9.5	4.4	199
All ages	19.1	2.9	1.6	3,476	20.5	4.2	.8	4,660

Measuring things, particularly nonmarket or uncompensated items such as the value of unpaid time or the "free rent" on an owned home, becomes more uncertain and potentially biased with older people. For example, for various tax reasons and because of inertia and emotional attachments, they tend to live in houses that are too large. But to add an imputed net rental value to their income exaggerates their economic well-being. They cannot eat or pay their medical bills with that imputed rent. If we want to value their housework or their hours of volunteer work, there is no market "opportunity cost" wage to start from, even apart from the selection biases in using that method with younger people, some of whom work.

Nor can we trust averages; inequality in income and wealth increases with age, and an average does not tell how many are below some threshold. More importantly, among younger people, those with low incomes or no assets are not likely to stay that way; the older people in those circumstances are likely to remain so. Comparing the fraction of poor in one year is comparing a set composed mostly of persistently poor older people with a set composed mostly of temporarily poor younger people. Asset means tests may be discouraging to younger people, but they can at least hope to build some savings later.

Measuring time use may also involve problems of comparability if there are differences in the intensity of work. With older people housework time tends to spread out and take up available hours while younger people may even be doing several things at the same time. The main issue, however, is not measurement and analysis but seeking ways to allow, encourage, and facilitate increased productive activity among the elderly.

What Affects Older Persons' Productive Activity?

We can model the forces affecting the productive activity of older persons in terms of incentives and disincentives or barriers. Five general propositions apply:

1. Multiple incentives are better than solitary ones, and it is essential that all the barriers and most of the disincentives be removed. Both the incentives and the barriers range from the monetary through the more broadly economic to the psychological-sociological (altruism, social roles, inertia, and

social obligations), and then to physical conditions (health and the physical environment).

2. Changing people's behavior is difficult at best and becomes increasingly so as people get older. A lifetime of habit and becoming accustomed to one set of roles and environments does not predispose an individual to venturesome changes, and yet small one-thing-at-a-time changes are unlikely to provide substantial rewards.

3. Ordinary paid work in the usual marketplace is the least promising activity to expect older people to expand. Care for themselves and others is probably the most likely, with various forms of semimarket activity (growing food, sewing, or repairs) probably somewhere in the middle.

4. Money incentives may well be less important, and affective rewards more important, among older people. Both, however, are required.

5. The disparity among individuals in the capacity to produce, relative to the level of needs, becomes greater with age. Some people stay healthy, accumulate assets, and acquire multiple useful skills while others become increasingly dependent. For all our concern with incentives, it is crucial to remember that most differences in productive activity are the involuntary result of life histories, health, and an individual's particular environment. Attempts to increase economic incentives can result in rewarding the fortunate and punishing the unfortunate.

The terms "unpaid" and "voluntary" are imprecise. We need to distinguish market transactions—that is, paid labor—from (1) productive effort with expectations of some reciprocal benefits, (2) productive effort with direct benefits (e.g., home production and repairs), and (3) productive effort with no expectation or contract for anything in return (pure altruism). Any of these three can be in an individual or two-person context or through an organization such as a church or volunteer group.

There are serious difficulties with the notion of increasing the altruistic unpaid work of older people. If there is no reciprocity or return benefit, the burden is likely to be quite unequal because of the unequal capacities and preferences of older people. And there are limits to reciprocal (bilateral) mutual help arrangements, just as there are to any barter arrangement—the necessity for each pair to stay in balance severely restricts activity. (For example, one report on an experiment in encouraging shared housing found relatively little permanent success; more people wanted to share their homes than wanted to live in someone else's (Pritchard, 1983). Multilateral trade is unquestionably more complex, requiring agreements, prices, and money (or some substitute), but it vastly increases trade.

It seems likely that compatibility and equitable financial arrangements are much more difficult with very small numbers of people than with larger groups. A larger group or community can have more special skills available, can afford to invest its members' time in working out equitable and efficient arrangements, and can achieve economies of scale. It can also allow subgroups of friends to provide social support to each other without insisting that everyone get along swimmingly with everyone else.

When we combine the need for multilateral arrangements with the disparity in abilities and needs among individuals, it becomes apparent that we need a combination of savings accumulation and insurance to make the system work. Each individual would contribute to a fund that would then pay for the involuntary needs of some individuals as a form of insurance but would also accumulate a substantial sum. (Younger individuals would pay more, on the average, than they took out knowing that later they, as an age group, would get more paid out than the fund was taking in from them.) Individuals would then receive compensation for helping one another, directly from the helped person if the need was voluntary but from the insurance fund if it was involuntary (e.g., nursing during illness, etc.).

Implicit in all this is an attempt to separate efficiency from equity considerations, to focus not on changing the amount of redistribution or subsidy but on opening up a wider variety of opportunities and alternatives. There is much to be said for distinguishing economically self-sustaining arrangements from subsidies, bribes, and coercions. Indeed, the usual tax-break methods of encouragement are particularly likely to be inequitable among the elderly; those kinds of benefits will probably be limited to those with high tax rates. A good test of any program is whether it is viable on its own or whether some funds are needed, such as a temporary development fund to start an "infant industry" or a loan rather than a permanent flow of subsidy. For some kinds of new living arrangements to facilitate efficient self- and mutual help among the aged, what appears to be needed are some small development funds to assist the first attempts and export the successful mechanism (not rules, but rules for developing rules). Another important method is the use of nonamortized loans; older people may not always need or want to be accumulating further equity in their last years. There is an important difference between a project that covers its own costs, including interest on loans, and one that is subsidized or one that mimics condominiums for the young intent on saving taxes while building equities.

It seems likely that removing all the barriers to more productive activity among the elderly will do a great deal of good. Because many things can inhibit the process or cause changes in the issues at hand, we need coordinated, multifaceted, comprehensive programs that solve all the problems. Furthermore, because many of the problems will arise in midstream, what we need are not fixed projects but the creation of new viable institutions or communities that with the full participation of the members solve each problem as it comes along. Indeed, the very solving of those problems may be the most productive thing some of our elderly could be doing.

WHERE DOES THIS LEAVE US?

Are we then back to our "common pleas" for more research and more data? Yes, indeed, we are—but as preparation for field trials of new societal arrangements. Even if the scare statistics about the ratio of total population to employed workers are misleading and exaggerated, we do face a much larger and older retired population and potential further increases in life expectancy. The very economic security and medical insurance that may well have increased that life expectancy is now an object of controversy.

It seems likely that paid employment will remain scarce and will require younger, better trained, more flexible workers, even though the demands for low-tech products like nursing care and other services grow because we have no efficient "affordable" ways to provide those services. The greatest potential for productive activity among older people may well be in self-help and mutual help and in activities formerly performed largely by volunteers. This does not mean that we should expect great increases in unpaid activity among older people but perhaps that we should facilitate and provide at least some compensation for many of these activities.

A first step would be assessment of the "human capital" of skills and experience among the retired and those soon to be retired. They are unlikely to provide good direct forecasts of how they would respond to new opportunities and incentives, but we can at least infer their capabilities.

A second step might well be some field trials (a better term than experiments) facilitating the formation of communities that would work out the physical, economic, and insurance-type arrangements to encourage all kinds of productive activities within a framework allowing maximum choice, freedom, rewards, etc. Take the case of the care of the sick and temporarily disabled, or the partially permanently disabled. Currently, in about half the cases this care seems to take place in extremely expensive hospitals and nursing homes where costs are often out of control. Or sometimes this work is performed by a spouse at considerable physical, emotional, and sometimes financial costs (since the insurance schemes do not cover most of it). Extended families only rarely can be expected to help because they tend to be scattered and have their own children to care for. Natural communities do not develop. Indeed, most older people see their network of social support withering as their friends die, and the isolation in single-family homes does not encourage the development of new social support networks.

We know that a mixture of economic incentives, combined with inertia and emotional attachment, makes staying in the family home attractive unless alternatives appear that offer a solution to several problems at once:

- protection against outliving one's savings;
- protection against being financially devastated by a medical or other emergency;
- protection against inflation;
- development and maintenance of a social support network;
- provision of opportunities for increased productive activity in a variety of ways; and
- provision of opportunities for social and economic interaction in a community but maintaining privacy when desired and control over some indoor and outdoor space.

No one-at-a-time changes or experiments to isolate the effects of only one thing will do us much good in finding solutions to these problems. We must take some longer leaps, and in that kind of activity, preliminary research will be of little help.

SUMMARY

We have shown that there is little reason to expect increased productive activity among the elderly under the present system of living arrangements, tax laws, and expectations, particularly the expectation that some work we do must be performed with little or no compensation. Furthermore, attempting to rely on tax incentives or coercions like changing the retirement age threaten to punish the unfortunate or benefit the fortunate instead of changing behavior. Increasing options and reducing barriers may well be important, particularly if new arrangements provide many different benefits and solve many different problems all at the same time. It seems unlikely that piecemeal approaches or rigid experiments that do not have built-in adjustment mechanisms will do more than prove what cannot work. Further research might reduce the risks of field trials of comprehensive new arrangements, but for this to succeed, risks will have to be taken. Finally, we suggest that the design of any new plan or system should emphasize economically viable alternatives, separating subsidies and income redistributions from attempts to improve the efficiency of our social and economic arrangements.

REFERENCES

Barfield, Richard, and James Morgan. 1969. *Early Retirement, The Decision and the Experience.* Ann Arbor, Mich.: Institute for Social Research.

Hill, Martha S. Forthcoming. "Patterns of Time Use." In *Time Use, Goods, and Well Being.* Edited by F. Thomas Juster and Frank Stafford.

Morgan, Leslie A. 1983. "Intergenerational Financial Support: Retirement-Age Males, 1972–1975." *The Gerontologist* 3(April): 160–166.

Morgan, James N. 1980. "Retirement in Prospect and Retrospect." In *Five Thousand American Families: Patterns of Economic Progress.* Vol. 8. Ann Arbor, Mich.: Institute for Social Research.

Morgan, James N. 1983. "The Redistribution of Income by Families and Institutions and Family Help Patterns." In *Five Thousand American Families: Patterns of Economic Progress.* Vol. 10. Edited by Greg J. Duncan. Ann Arbor, Mich.: Institute for Social Research.

Morgan, James N. Forthcoming (1985). "Effects of Changing Family Composition on Housework and Food Consumption." *Journal of Consumer Research.*

Morgan, James N. Forthcoming. "The Role of Time in the Measurement of Transfers and Well-Being." In *Conference on Social Accounting for Transfer Payments.* Edited by Marilyn Moon. Cambridge, Mass.: National Bureau of Economic Research.

Morgan, James N., Ismail A. Sirageldin, and Nancy Baerwaldt. 1966. *Productive Americans.* Ann Arbor, Mich.: Institute for Social Research.

Morgan, James N., Richard F. Dye, and Judith H. Hybels. 1979. *Results from Two National Surveys of Philanthropic Activity.* Research Report Series. Ann Arbor, Mich.: Institute for Social Research. Reprint. Commission on Private Philanthropy and Public Needs. 1977. *Research Paper Series.* Vol. 1. Washington, D.C.: U.S. Treasury Department.

Parnes, Herbert S., et al. 1970. "From the Middle to the Later Years: Longitudinal Studies in the Preretirement and Postretirement Experiences of Men." In *The Retirement Experience.* Columbus, Ohio: Center for Human Resource Research, Ohio State University.

Pritchard, David C. 1983. "The Art of Matchmaking: A Close Study of Shared Housing." *The Gerontologist* 23 (April 1983): 174–179.

Streib, Gordon F., and Clement J. Schneider 1971. *Retirement in American Society: Impact and Process.* Ithaca, N.Y.: Cornell University Press.

Sociodemographic Aspects of Future Unpaid Productive Roles

George C. Myers, Kenneth G. Manton, and Helena Bacellar

In some respects the appraisal of forecasts puts a greater burden on the policymaker than the original task of forecasting itself. The accuracy of current forecasts is of course yet to be determined. Evaluation of the methodology of various forecasts may require technical sophistication at least as great as, and perhaps greater than, that of the specialist in forecasting. Yet the policymaker is rarely a specialist in forecasting techniques, nor usually an authority on the phenomena being projected (Ascher, 1978: 1–2).

The purpose of this paper is to provide a background for consideration of the sociodemographic factors relating to unpaid productive roles in an aging society. The prospective nature of this task requires that use be made of projections or other analytic procedures that attempt to gauge the nature of the population structure in the decades ahead. This is a challenging task in itself, but it is made even more difficult by the task of determining the relevant aspects of a concept as diffuse as unpaid productive roles.

The National Institute on Aging's *Report of the National Research on Aging Planning Panel* (1982) identified four types of

George C. Myers and Kenneth G. Manton are affiliated with the Center for Demographic Studies, Duke University, Durham, North Carolina. Helena Bacellar is a member of the Department of Sociology, Duke University, Durham, North Carolina.

activities that do not involve direct wage remuneration: (1) work activities contributed without payment to a family farm or business, or work undertaken on a do-it-yourself basis; (2) involvement in voluntary organizations—civic, church, social, and so forth; (3) mutual help provided to (or by) family, friends, and neighbors; and (4) self-help that encompasses care of one's own person or one's immediate living space. The report emphasized that relatively little is known about the nature and value of such roles for individuals and for society, about the mechanisms that promote such activities, and about the obstacles and constraints that prevent such activities from being pursued on a larger scale.

Although considerable research has been devoted to paid employment among older persons (for example, studies on the impact of relaxing mandatory retirement laws, delaying early retirement decisions, the effect of earnings tests), relatively little attention has been given to *unpaid* activities and the design of interventions that might alter the conditions affecting such activities. Thus, emphasis has been placed almost totally on the monetary benefits of activities among older persons. Virtually ignored has been the impact of such behavior on the general well-being of older persons and the impact it might have on the society at large (Rosow, 1976). Adopting a broadened perspective, these varied notions can be encapsulated under the general concept of "vintage capital," by which we mean anything that enhances a person's power to engage in useful activities (i.e., producing goods and services).

The different types of unpaid activities reflect on the interplay between formal and informal roles and the relative status that may or may not adhere to such roles. Older age is generally viewed as a stage in the life course in which formal and perhaps informal role deficits occur. The most noticeable role change involves formal work roles, but other roles also may be lost, dropped, or modified. Unpaid activities can be viewed as alternatives to paid work and as adaptations to changing life conditions. The dimensions of such activities, however, are even more complex in nature. For example, in addition to the formal or informal nature of such roles, there is variation in the types of activities that might be pursued, for whom they are intended, the level of activity required, the reward structures (which may sometimes include partial remuneration), and the nature of the environments in which the activities take place. So, too, attention must be given to both suppliers (providers) and consumers (users) of such activities. (In the case of self-help, of course, these are the same person.) The activities also may include younger persons as well as older persons, although the main emphasis of this paper is on older persons. Finally, it should be noted that there are role requirements attached to being a user as well as to being a provider. While it is often assumed that persons in need of care are willing to accept such attention, this may sometimes not be the case. Nor, for that matter, can it be assumed that persons fully capable of engaging in activities necessarily are motivated to do so.

We have dwelled at some length on various conceptual issues because they are relevant in important ways to the main concern of this paper. The general demographic situation provides a context for determining the extent to which such activities are of societal importance (i.e., demand)—as for example in determining potential suppliers and consumers. The sociodemographic characteristics of these population aggregates obviously command attention, especially in terms of changes that may occur over time. But the selection of which characteristics might fruitfully be examined is difficult because so little is known empirically about the phenomenon in question. Even in areas that have been researched, such as participation in voluntary associations, philanthropy, political involvement—the correlates of activity and sociodemographic characteristics are sketchy and inconclusive, especially when the subject pertains to older persons. Moreover, it is likely to be the case that the greater the empirical knowledge about these relationships, the more complex they will become with respect to the specificity of the activities in question, the interaction among the characteristics of providers and users, and the likelihood of intercohort patterns changing over time.

To provide a first slice of this potentially rich pie, we have elected in this paper to present some information about sociodemographic characteristics of the population that could possibly influence the levels of nonpaid productive activities in the future. We have relied upon existing national population projections and selected analytical studies in this effort. In so doing, issues are raised about both the relevance, technical suitability, and reliability of such projective exercises. The last section of this paper devotes specific attention to a review of the current state of these activities.

The task before us, then, is not to test any hypotheses but rather to examine a limited set of sociodemographic characteristics of the total population and older segments of the population. We suspect that such characteristics of the population as the age structure, sex composition, labor force participation, education, household structure and marital status, kinship structure, and health may be related to providers and users. In a real sense, we are actually only considering potential pools of such persons. However, by examining these sociodemographic characteristics of populations projected into the future, we learn not only about possible outcomes but about past trends, because most forecasts are based on known trends that are "projected" into the future. We can project certain features of the older population with some assurance, mainly because they are dependent on only one or a few parameters (numerical counts, age, sex composition); other features are more difficult to forecast (marital status, labor force participation, health). Thus, there is a conceptual leap being made in such an effort that exemplifies Ascher's comment at the opening of the paper. The difficult tasks lie not only in the act of forecasting but in interpreting the results and drawing issues of policy concern from them.

PROJECTIONS OF MAJOR POPULATION CHARACTERISTICS

Table 1, which is a detailed accounting of the age and sex distribution of the population, is included here to provide the most recent (1982) Bureau of the Census projections. While the projections are intended mainly for reference, they do enable us to see how the U.S. population will continue to grow in size over the period to 2050 and then stabilize. In addition, the figures reveal shifts in population structure. Females predominate over males, both in the aggregate and at ages over 25 currently, but at later ages in subsequent years. This change reflects on assumptions that have been made about changes in mortality differentials by sex, and possibly migration, which rest in the technical details of the forecast. Finally, and most relevant for our purposes, the figures for the older population, which we refer to generally in this paper as all persons 65 years of age and over, show the rapid growth of this subpopulation—in numbers and as a proportion of the total population. From 11.4 percent of the population in 1980, it is expected to increase to 17.3 percent by the year 2020.

The most recent projections reveal considerably greater growth in both the numbers and the proportions of older persons in the population than was true for the last "official" projections in 1977. This reflects mainly the modified forecasts of mortality reductions at all ages, including the older ages. Table 2 provides an overview of some relevant features of these projections of the older population to the year 2080.

The number of older persons will increase at a fairly modest pace for the rest of this century and then will increase steadily until the baby-boom generation reaches age 65 in the period 2012 to 2025. By 2020 the aged population is projected to be 51.4 million, or about 17 percent of the total population. The age distribution of the aged population fluctuates, as might be expected, depending mainly on the size of entering cohorts. These structural dynamics have direct relevance for the issues raised in this paper and probably have greater importance than the size of the aggregate older population per se. What is particularly note-worthy is the increased size of the very old group, 85 years of age and over, which by the year 2000 will constitute 14.1 percent of the total aged population. The sex ratio of this population group reveals an extremely high proportion of females—over two females for each male—although these ratios will become less extreme over time.

A simple means of assessing structural shifts in population is by the use of ratios relating one age grouping to another; these are sometimes referred to as dependency ratios. The ratios of the so-called active population (20 to 64 years of age) to the total aged population decline sharply to the year 2020, continuing to decrease to the year 2080.

Another ratio that is of interest relates the younger older persons to the very old (that is, persons aged 65 to 74 to those 85 and over). This ratio drops sharply to the year 2000; it then rises, but drops again to less than two younger older persons to a single very old person in 2050 and 2080. Finally, a ratio that is some-times called a familial aged dependency ratio, which relates older persons to the population 45 to 49 years of age, can be calculated. This group might be thought of as the cohort of children related to persons reaching ages 65 to 69. These ratios also decline through the year 2000, rise sharply by 2020, and slowly continue to increase thereafter.

The characteristics of the elderly population portrayed in Table 2 are commonly noted in overviews of the aged population, but their importance cannot be overemphasized. In considering both demand and supply issues relating to unpaid productive roles, these characteristics clearly show the profound aging process that is under way, the full impact of which will not be felt until the baby-boom generation reaches old age. But the sanguine attitude that sometimes prevails regarding trends for the next few decades up to that point of explosion in the next century encourages a vision of a "breathing spell" that is probably unwarranted. In fact, the aged population will grow steadily in the rest of this century while net additions to the older population slowly decline in number, although they are still positive, to the year 2000. After that point the net additions increase at ever higher levels to the year 2012, when the growth further accelerates.

The aged population will continue to become older itself during the next three decades. The proportion of females is expected to increase for the total aged population and among the very old. To the extent that providers, in our terms, tend to be younger elderly women, the trends may suggest a potential increase in their supply. On the other hand, the preponderance of women at extremely old ages will probably lead to an increase on the demand side at least for the next 30 years. Finally, we should note one major characteristic of the older population—the high rate of turnover of individuals within the population. This turnover means that only 40 percent of the persons who are members of the older population at any point in time (say, 1980) would have been members of the population 10 years earlier. This high turnover not only affects the numbers in the population but may markedly alter its social and economic structure, due to changing characteristics of new entrants (cohorts), selective survival of the earlier older population, and some modifications in status through behavioral changes that may occur over time.

The population projections prepared by the Bureau of the Census have over time come to include an increasingly large set of alternative projections that reflect different assumptions made

TABLE 1   Estimates and Projections of the Population of the United States Including Armed Forces Overseas, by Age and Sex, 1980 to 2080 (Middle Series Projections) (in thousands)

	1980			1990			2000		
Age	Total	Male	Female	Total	Male	Female	Total	Male	Female
	227,658	110,834	116,824	249,657	121,518	128,139	267,955	130,491	137,464
0–4	16,448	8,413	8,036	19,198	9,827	9,371	17,626	9,022	8,604
5–9	16,595	8,482	8,108	18,591	9,511	9,080	18,758	9,599	9,159
10–14	18,227	9,318	8,919	16,773	8,586	8,207	19,519	9,986	7,532
15–19	21,123	10,758	10,365	16,968	8,670	8,299	18,943	9,681	9,262
20–24	21,605	10,900	10,705	18,580	9,433	9,137	17,145	8,723	8,422
25–29	19,763	9,876	9,887	21,522	10,878	10,645	17,396	8,804	8,592
30–34	17,824	8,845	8,979	22,007	11,814	10,992	19,019	9,580	9,439
35–39	14,126	6,966	9,162	20,001	9,933	10,068	21,753	10,925	10,828
40–44	11,752	5,760	5,992	17,846	8,799	9,048	21,990	10,941	11,049
45–49	11,047	5,372	5,675	13,980	6,831	7,148	19,763	9,739	10,024
50–54	11,684	5,612	5,075	11,422	5,519	5,903	17,356	8,457	8,899
55–59	11,619	5,483	6,136	10,433	4,954	5,479	13,280	6,363	6,917
60–64	10,134	4,691	5,443	10,618	4,917	5,701	10,487	4,909	5,578
65–69	8,805	3,914	4,891	9,996	4,458	5,538	9,096	4,108	4,989
70–74	6,843	2,873	3,970	8,039	3,405	4,634	8,581	3,665	4,196
75–79	4,815	1,856	2,959	6,260	2,436	3,825	7,295	2,869	4,426
80–84	2,972	1,030	1,942	4,089	1,420	2,669	5,023	1,771	3,252
85–89	1,541	483	1,058	2,157	642	1,515	3,025	907	2,118
90–94	575	164	411	849	211	638	1,355	335	1,020
95–99	130	34	96	253	55	198	438	90	348
100+	26	8	18	54	11	42	108	18	90
0–4	7.2%	7.6%	6.9%	7.7%	8.1%	7.3%	6.6%	6.9%	6.3%
5–9	7.3	7.6	6.9	7.4	7.8	7.1	7.0	7.4	6.7
10–14	8.0	8.4	7.6	6.7	7.1	6.4	7.3	7.7	6.9
15–19	9.3	9.7	8.9	6.8	7.1	6.5	7.1	7.4	6.7
20–24	9.5	9.8	9.2	7.4	7.8	7.1	6.4	6.7	6.1
25–29	8.7	8.9	8.5	8.6	9.0	8.3	6.5	6.7	6.3
30–34	7.8	8.0	7.7	8.8	9.1	8.6	7.1	7.3	6.9
35–39	6.2	6.3	6.1	8.0	8.2	7.9	8.1	8.4	7.9
40–44	5.2	5.2	5.1	7.1	7.2	7.1	8.2	8.4	8.0
45–49	4.8	4.8	4.8	5.6	5.6	5.6	7.4	7.5	7.3
50–54	5.1	5.1	5.2	4.6	4.5	4.6	6.5	6.5	6.5
55–59	5.1	4.9	5.2	4.2	4.1	4.3	5.0	4.9	5.0
60–64	4.4	4.2	4.6	4.3	4.0	4.4	3.9	3.8	4.1
65–69	3.9	3.5	4.2	4.0	3.7	4.3	3.4	3.1	3.6
70–74	3.0	2.6	3.4	3.2	2.8	3.6	3.2	2.8	3.6
75–79	2.1	1.7	2.5	2.5	2.0	3.0	2.7	2.2	3.2
80–84	1.3	0.9	1.7	1.6	1.2	2.1	1.9	1.4	2.4
85–89	0.7	0.4	0.9	0.9	0.5	1.2	1.1	0.7	1.5
90–94	0.3	0.1	0.4	0.3	0.2	0.5	0.5	0.3	0.7
95–99	0.1	0.0	0.1	0.1	1.4	0.2	0.2	0.0	0.3
100+	0.0	0.0	0.0	0.0	0.0	0.0	0.0	0.0	0.1
Total	100.0	100.0	100.0	100.0	100.0	100.0	100.0	100.0	100.0

SOURCE: U.S. Bureau of the Census. 1984. "Projections of the Population of the United States, by Age, Sex, and Race: 1983 to 2080." In *Current Population Reports.* Series P-25,

Age	2020 Total	Male	Female	2050 Total	Male	Female	2080 Total	Male	Female
	296,597	144,457	152,140	309,488	149,419	160,070	310,762	149,901	160,862
0–4	18,357	9,397	8,960	17,665	9,043	8,621	17,202	8,808	8,395
5–9	18,590	9,513	9,077	18,051	9,220	8,796	17,471	8,942	8,529
10–14	18,306	9,366	8,939	18,217	8,322	8,895	17,747	9,083	8,644
15–19	17,958	9,181	8,778	18,251	9,331	8,920	17,940	9,174	8,766
20–24	18,308	9,324	8,984	18,381	9,362	9,019	18,103	9,222	8,881
25–29	19,533	9,898	9,635	18,892	9,574	9,318	18,418	9,335	8,083
30–34	20,301	10,252	10,049	18,491	9,844	9,647	18,819	9,506	9,313
35–39	19,644	8,890	9,754	19,658	9,903	8,756	19,106	9,626	9,480
40–44	17,699	8,874	8,826	18,186	9,635	9,552	19,116	9,604	9,513
45–49	17,559	8,767	8,792	18,553	9,280	9,274	18,866	9,443	9,423
50–54	18,621	9,230	9,391	18,439	9,169	9,270	18,568	9,243	9,325
55–59	20,507	10,059	10,449	18,824	9,275	9,550	18,344	9,054	9,290
60–64	19,791	9,495	10,296	18,503	8,985	9,518	17,970	8,754	9,216
65–69	16,080	7,721	8,899	16,619	7,872	8,747	16,914	8,059	8,855
70–74	13,325	5,853	7,381	13,495	6,133	7,363	14,984	6,880	8,105
75–79	8,824	3,617	5,207	11,478	4,891	6,587	12,659	5,486	7,172
80–84	5,662	2,078	3,585	9,785	3,795	5,990	10,305	4,091	6,213
85–89	3,582	1,121	2,466	7,825	2,649	5,179	7,977	2,800	5,178
90–94	2,158	555	1,063	4,915	1,405	3,510	5,433	1,650	3,783
95–99	975	206	769	2,261	541	1,720	2,946	766	2,181
100+	361	60	301	1,029	191	838	1,870	372	1,498
0–4	6.2%	6.5%	5.9%	5.7%	6.1%	5.4%	5.5%	5.9%	5.2%
5–9	6.3	6.6	6.0	5.8	6.2	5.5	5.6	6.0	5.3
10–14	6.2	6.5	5.9	5.9	6.2	5.6	5.7	6.1	5.4
15–19	6.1	6.4	5.8	5.9	6.2	5.6	5.8	6.1	5.4
20–24	6.2	6.5	5.9	5.9	6.3	5.6	5.8	6.2	5.5
25–29	6.6	6.9	6.3	6.1	6.4	5.8	5.9	6.2	5.6
30–34	6.8	7.1	6.6	6.3	6.6	6.0	6.1	6.3	5.8
35–39	6.6	6.8	6.4	6.4	6.6	6.1	6.1	6.4	5.9
40–44	6.0	6.1	5.8	6.2	6.4	6.0	6.2	6.4	5.9
45–49	5.9	6.1	5.8	6.0	6.2	5.8	6.1	6.3	5.9
50–54	6.3	6.4	6.2	6.0	6.1	5.8	6.0	6.2	5.8
55–59	6.9	7.0	6.9	6.1	6.2	6.0	5.9	6.0	5.8
60–64	6.7	6.6	6.8	6.0	6.0	5.9	5.8	5.8	5.7
65–69	5.6	5.3	5.8	5.4	5.3	5.5	5.4	5.4	5.5
70–74	4.5	4.1	4.9	4.4	4.1	4.6	4.8	4.6	5.0
75–79	3.0	2.5	3.4	3.7	3.3	4.1	4.1	3.7	4.5
80–84	1.9	1.4	2.4	3.2	2.5	3.7	3.3	2.7	3.9
85–89	1.2	0.8	1.6	2.5	1.8	3.2	2.6	1.9	3.2
90–94	0.7	0.4	1.1	1.6	0.9	2.2	1.7	1.1	2.4
95–99	0.3	0.1	0.5	0.7	0.4	1.1	0.9	0.5	1.4
100+	0.1	0.0	0.2	0.3	0.1	0.5	0.6	0.2	0.9
Total	100.0	100.0	100.0	100.0	100.0	100.0	100.0	100.0	100.0

No. 952. Washington, D.C.: U.S. Government Printing Office. Unpublished data were used for ages 85–100+ in 1980.

TABLE **2** Selected Statistics on Population 65 Years of Age and Over, United States 1980–2080 (Middle Series Projections)

	Year				
	1980	2000	2020	2050	2080
Total population (in thousands)	25,708	34,912	51,422	67,407	73,089
Percentage of aged	11.3	13.0	17.3	21.8	23.5
Ages–number (in thousands)					
65–69	8,805	9,096	16,620	16,619	16,914
70–74	6,843	8,581	13,235	13,495	14,984
75–79	4,815	7,295	8,824	11,478	12,659
80–84	2,972	5,023	5,662	9,785	10,306
85–89	1,541	3,025	3,587	7,825	7,977
90–94	575	1,355	2,158	4,915	5,433
95–99	130	438	975	2,261	2,946
100+	26	108	361	1,029	1,870
Ages–percentage	100.0	100.0	100.0	100.0	100.0
65–69	34.2	26.0	32.3	24.7	23.1
70–74	26.6	24.6	25.7	20.0	20.5
75–79	18.7	20.9	17.2	17.0	17.3
80–84	11.6	14.4	11.0	14.5	14.1
85–89	6.0	8.7	7.0	11.6	10.9
90–94	2.2	3.9	4.2	7.3	7.4
95–99	0.5	1.2	1.9	3.4	4.0
100+	0.1	0.3	0.7	1.5	2.6
Sex ratio	67.5	65.0	70.2	68.8	70.0
65–69	80.0	82.3	86.8	90.0	91.0
70–74	72.4	74.6	79.3	83.3	84.9
75–79	62.7	64.8	69.5	74.3	76.5
80–84	53.0	54.5	58.0	63.4	65.9
85–89	45.7	42.8	45.5	51.1	54.1
90–94	39.9	32.8	34.6	40.0	43.6
95–99	35.1	25.9	26.8	31.5	35.1
100+	44.4	20.0	19.9	22.8	24.8
Percent nonwhite of total aged	9.3	10.9	13.8	19.1	23.5
Population structure ratios					
20–64/20	1.79	2.11	2.35	2.36	2.38
20–64/65+	5.04	4.53	3.34	2.52	2.29
20–64/20–65+	1.32	1.44	1.38	1.22	1.17
65–74/85+	6.88	3.59	4.22	1.88	1.75
65–79/45–49	1.85	1.26	2.20	2.24	2.36

SOURCE: U.S. Bureau of the Census. 1984. "Projections of the Population of the United States, by Age, Sex, and Race: 1983 to 2080." In *Current Population Reports.* Series P-25, No. 952. Washington, D.C.: U.S. Government Printing Office. Unpublished data were used for ages 85–100+ in 1980.

about future levels of fertility, mortality, and migration. Whereas mortality assumptions may affect the numbers and percentage of the aged population over both the short and long terms, variations in fertility and migration mainly operate in the long term on the numbers of older persons and on both time frames with respect to the relative proportions of the older population. For the 1984 projections, we can illustrate this effect on the projected numbers of older persons by examining 3 out of the 30 series produced: the lowest, middle (which has been presented earlier), and highest series. The lowest series reflects a low fertility assumption of 1.6 births per woman, a low net migration of 250,000 persons, and high mortality. The middle series reflects middle assumptions on fertility with 1.9 births per woman, a net migration of 450,000 persons per year, and middle mortality. Finally, the highest series reflects high fertility assumptions of 2.3 births per woman, a high net migration of 750,000 persons, and low mortality. On the other hand, with middle assumptions on fertility (1.9 births per woman) and net migration (450,000 persons), high mortality assumptions reflect a life expectancy at birth of 77.4 years in the year 2080. For the middle and low mortality assumptions, life expectancy at birth in the year 2080 rises from 81.0 to 85.9 years. Table 3 shows how these assumptions affect the older population.

In the middle and high series, there is continuous growth of the population 65 years of age and over through the 100-year period. In the lowest series the size of the aged population increases and then declines after 2040. If we consider the extreme values as providing certain levels of confidence about the middle series, then the range of possible error increases over time, with the difference between the low and high series reaching over 60 million by the year 2080. In terms of the impact of these extreme series on the proportion of older persons, the low series would produce 13.1 percent of the population aged in 2000 and 25.6 percent in 2080, while comparable figures for the high series would be 12.9 and 20.7 percent.

Although we may feel fairly confident that the middle series represents a set of reasonable (if perhaps somewhat low on the life expectancy improvement) assumptions, we also must recognize that the possibilities of being in error increase over time. Nonetheless, even under the least favorable assumptions, the numbers of older persons will more than double in size in the

TABLE 3   Variations in Alternative Projections of Population 65 Years of Age and Older, United States, 2000–2080 (in thousands)

Number of Persons 65 and Over	Year				
	2000	2020	2040	2060	2080
Lowest series	33,621	47,139	58,116	54,871	49,035
Middle series	34,921	51,422	66,988	70,081	73,089
Highest series	36,246	56,332	78,558	90,808	109,895
Difference (high–low)	2,625	9,193	20,442	35,937	60,860
Percentage of difference (low–middle)	−3.7	−8.3	−13.2	−21.7	−32.9
Percentage of difference (high–middle)	+3.8	+9.5	+17.3	+29.6	+50.4

SOURCE: U.S. Bureau of the Census. 1984. "Projections of the Population of the United States, by Age, Sex, and Race: 1983 to 2080." In *Current Population Reports*. Series P-25, No. 952. Washington, D.C.: U.S. Government Printing Office.

next 50 years, and the proportion of the aged population will closely approach 20 percent. The presentation of these figures does give ample evidence about the fragility of efforts to project populations and the importance of the basic assumptions that enter into their derivation.

GEOGRAPHIC DISTRIBUTION

In addition to the size of the older population and its composition by age and sex, it is also important to assess current and future changes in its spatial distribution. Table 4 provides projections to the year 2000, which unfortunately is as far as the current projections extend in time. In terms of total population, the projections reveal an increasing proportion of the U.S. population residing in the South and West and a declining share in the Northeast and in the North Central states. The trends for the proportion of older persons follow comparable patterns, although the Northeast will continue to have a proportionately greater share of older persons and the West will continue to be somewhat underrepresented by older persons. More than a third of the older population will continue to be found in the South.

The lower panel of Table 4 provides greater age detail for the regions. The figures emphasize the considerable aging of the aged population itself to the year 2000. The larger percentage gains in the population 85 years and over in the South and West are particularly noteworthy. The Northeast, which has had the highest proportions of these oldest persons, also will continue to show increasing numbers of the very old. These changing features of geographic distribution for different age groups provide a strong argument for greater attention to the distribution of programs and service support among the major regions of the country and undoubtedly among selected states within these regions. These dynamics of redistribution are often neglected in considering changing patterns of demand for the U.S. population as a whole.

LABOR FORCE PARTICIPATION

Forecasts of labor force participation up to the year 2000 have recently been prepared by the Bureau of Labor Statistics as part of general economic projections made to 1995. These labor force participation rates are then simply applied to projected census figures to determine the size of the labor force at future dates.

The figures for 1982 in Table 5 provide an indication of current patterns in labor force participation. Rates for males, which are higher than those for females at all ages, peak at ages 35 to 44 and then decline sharply after age 55. In earlier estimates for 1982, it was shown that only slightly more than a quarter of men were in the labor force between ages 65 to 69, a level that has shown a precipitous decline in the past few decades. The participation rates of females tend to follow the same pattern as men but always at lower levels. In fact, rates for women are less than half the levels for men at the older ages, which reflects earlier cohort differences in participation for the most part.

The projections to the years 1990 and 1995 show that slight declines are expected in the rates of participation for men at most ages. However, a continuation of the rapid change for women toward greater involvement in the labor force up to age 60 is viewed as likely. Rates for males are still above those for women at all ages in 1990 and 1995. At ages over 60 the participation rates are expected to decline for males and to remain fairly stable for females. Thus, the work patterns that have emerged in the past few decades are forecasted to continue, with proportionately more women participating throughout the life course than was

TABLE 4 Projections of the Population 65 Years of Age and Over, by Region, United States, 1980–2000

	Population (in thousands)			Percentage of Distribution			Percentage of Change		
	1980	1990	2000	1980	1990	2000	1980–1990	1990–2000	1980–2000
U.S. total population	226,505	249,203	267,462	100.0	100.0	100.0	10.0	7.3	18.1
Northeast	49,137	48,423	46,401	21.7	19.4	17.4	−1.5	−4.2	−5.6
North central	58,854	60,265	59,714	26.0	24.2	22.3	2.4	−0.9	1.5
South	75,349	87,594	98,828	33.3	35.2	37.0	16.3	12.8	31.2
West	43,165	52,920	62,519	19.1	21.2	23.4	22.6	18.1	44.8
U.S. total population, 65+	25,544	31,799	35,036	100.0	100.0	100.0	24.5	10.2	37.2
Northeast, 65+	6,072	6,912	6,828	23.8	21.7	19.5	13.8	−1.2	12.4
North central, 65+	6,691	7,650	7,763	26.2	24.1	22.2	14.4	1.4	16.0
South, 65+	8,484	11,403	13,582	33.2	35.9	36.9	34.4	19.1	60.1
West, 65+	4,298	5,829	6,684	16.8	18.3	22.4	35.6	17.7	59.7
U.S. total population, 65+	25,544	31,799	35,036	100.0	100.0	100.0	24.5	10.2	37.2
65–69	8,781	10,006	9,110	34.4	31.5	26.0	14.0	−9.0	3.7
70–74	6,797	8,048	8,583	26.6	25.3	24.5	15.5	6.6	26.3
75–79	4,793	6,224	7,242	18.8	19.6	20.7	29.8	16.4	39.3
80–84	2,934	4,060	4,965	11.5	12.8	14.2	38.4	22.3	69.2
85+	2,240	3,461	5,136	8.8	10.9	14.6	54.5	48.4	129.3

Northeast, 65+	6,072	6,912	6,828	100.0	100.0	100.0	13.8	-1.2	12.4
65–69	2,068	2,150	1,705	34.0	31.1	25.0	4.0	-20.7	-17.6
70–74	1,595	1,737	1,648	26.3	25.1	24.1	8.4	-5.1	3.3
75–79	1,139	1,336	1,400	18.8	19.3	20.5	17.3	4.8	22.9
80–84	724	885	992	12.0	12.8	14.5	22.2	12.1	37.0
85+	546	804	1,084	9.0	11.6	15.9	47.2	34.8	98.5
North Central, 65+	6,691	7,656	7,763	100.0	100.0	100.0	14.4	1.4	16.0
65–69	2,220	2,341	1,967	33.2	30.6	25.3	5.4	-16.0	-11.4
70–74	1,737	1,896	1,859	26.0	24.8	23.9	9.2	-2.0	7.0
75–79	1,268	1,499	1,589	19.0	19.6	20.5	18.2	6.0	25.3
80–84	818	1,019	1,140	12.2	13.3	14.7	24.6	11.9	39.4
85+	649	901	1,209	9.7	11.8	15.6	38.8	34.2	86.3
South, 65+	8,484	11,403	13,582	100.0	100.0	100.0	36.4	19.1	60.1
65–69	2,980	3,622	3,616	35.1	31.8	26.6	21.5	-0.2	21.3
70–74	2,330	2,930	3,417	27.5	25.7	25.2	25.8	16.6	46.6
75–79	1,599	2,269	2,831	18.8	19.9	20.8	41.9	24.8	77.0
80–84	911	1,466	1,875	10.7	12.7	13.8	58.7	29.7	105.8
85+	664	1,137	1,844	7.8	10.0	13.6	71.2	62.2	177.7
West, 65+	4,298	5,829	6,684	100.0	100.0	100.0	35.6	17.7	59.7
65–69	1,514	1,893	1,823	35.2	32.5	26.6	25.0	-3.7	20.4
70–74	1,134	1,486	1,660	26.4	25.5	24.2	31.0	11.7	46.4
75–79	787	1,120	1,422	18.3	19.2	20.7	42.3	27.0	80.7
80–84	482	711	959	11.2	12.2	14.0	47.5	34.9	99.0
85+	380	619	1,000	8.8	10.6	14.6	62.9	61.6	163.2

SOURCE: U.S. Bureau of the Census. 1983. "Provisional Projections of the Population of the United States by Age and Sex: 1980 to 2000." In *Current Population Reports*. Series P-25, No. 917. Washington, D.C.: U.S. Government Printing Office.

TABLE 5 Labor Force Participation Rates by Age
and Sex, United States, 1982–1995 (Middle Series
Projections)

Age	1982	1990	1995
Males			
16–19	56.37	62.3	62.9
20–24	84.9	84.4	84.1
25–29	94.7	92.9	92.3
30–34		94.5	93.9
35–39	95.3	96.2	95.8
40–44		94.8	94.8
45–49	91.2	93.4	93.2
50–54		88.7	88.4
55–59	70.2	78.1	76.7
60–64		52.8	50.5
65–69		23.3	21.2
70–74	17.8	15.0	13.8
75+		6.9	6.3
Total:			
16–75+	76.6	76.5	76.1
Females			
16–19	51.4	56.8	58.2
20–24	69.8	78.1	82.0
25–29	68.0	78.5	82.2
30–34		77.8	81.3
35–39	68.0	78.0	82.0
40–44		79.2	83.5
45–49	61.6	69.2	71.3
50–54		64.5	67.3
55–59	41.8	51.1	51.9
60–64		32.1	32.1
65–69		15.1	15.2
70–74	7.9	7.2	7.1
75+		2.2	2.0
Total:			
16–75+	52.6	58.3	60.3

SOURCE: Bureau of Labor Statistics. 1984. *Employment Projections for 1995.* Bulletin 2197, Appendix A-1. Washington, D.C.: U.S. Government Printing Office.

true previously. Proportionately fewer older males and about the same proportion of older females are expected to be in the labor force.

The National Institute on Aging (1984) has developed longer-term projections to the year 2055 from its macroeconomic-demographic model, projections that permit an examination of the size of the labor force in broad age categories (Table 6).

Although the labor force as a whole is expected to increase by over 28 million workers by the year 2000, the number of older persons in the labor force is projected to decline, notably among men. Although the number of females in the labor force will continue at fairly stable levels until the middle of the next century, the number of older males after 2000 is expected to increase. This is due largely to the increase in their total numbers, not to the proportions employed. What is striking about these projections, which of course represent only one possible scenario, is the very modest impact that employment of older persons has upon the labor force as a whole.

From a supply point of view, the pool of women younger than 60 years of age and potentially available for service to others is expected to decline to the year 2000. On the other hand, both

TABLE **6** Projected Labor Force Participation by Age and Sex, 1980–2055 (in millions)

	1980	2000	2020	2050	2055
Male					
16–24	12.1	11.1	11.2	12.8	13.4
25–64	44.4	55.9	56.4	57.0	57.3
65 +	1.9	1.8	22.9	3.4	3.9
Total	58.4	68.8	90.5	73.2	74.6
Female					
16–24	9.7	10.8	11.5	12.6	13.2
25–64	28.2	45.1	52.9	57.2	58.2
65 +	1.1	1.1	1.1	1.2	1.4
Total	39.0	57.0	65.5	71.0	72.8

	Rate of Growth (average annual percentage)		
	1980–2020	2020–2055	1980–2055
Male			
16–24	−0.06	0.36	0.15
25–64	0.60	0.04	0.34
65 +	1.06	0.85	0.96
Total	0.49	0.14	0.32
Female			
16–24	0.42	1.39	0.41
25–64	1.57	0.27	0.97
65 +	0.00	0.69	0.32
Total	1.30	0.30	0.83

SOURCE: National Institute on Aging. 1984. *Macroeconomic-Demographic Model.* Table 1–7. Washington, D.C.: U.S. Government Printing Office.

women and men out of the labor force at older ages will be numerically and proportionately greater.

The effects of various changes in retirement behavior, coupled with and generated by changes in federal legislation (especially related to Social Security) on work levels, have been examined in projection studies by the Urban Institute (Wertheimer and Zedlewski, 1980; Hendricks and Storey, 1981) and ICF Incorporated (Anderson and McNaught, 1982). They permit us to see how such enactments, some of which are already in place, might influence labor force participation.

Projections made by the Urban Institute (Wertheimer and Zedlewski, 1980) utilized the microsimulation model DYNASIM to examine 1990 labor force participation rates under a high and a low scenario. Essentially, the two series differ in terms of early or late departure from the labor force. In Table 7, work status and annual hours worked are examined for males and females in different age groups. Under the low series, which relates closely to present conditions, there is a clear decline in labor force participation and corresponding decreases in mean hours worked for males at all ages and for females at age intervals 65 years and over. The high series effects mainly occur at ages 62 to 64 for males, especially in the amount of full-time employment. At 65 years and over the levels are only slightly elevated for mean hours worked by workers, but the proportions of individuals who have retired are roughly comparable to levels in 1977. The same impact is found for females.

Another application of the microsimulation model by Hendricks and Storey (1981) has examined different assumptions regarding the effect of mandatory retirement policies on labor force participation rates of men in the year 2000. Inasmuch as some of these changes have already been implemented, the results are interesting to examine in terms of their effect on working levels through the ages 60 to 70. Under the existing change that raised the minimum mandatory retirement age to 70, the increase in male labor force participation was projected as minimal in the year 2000 for the 60 to 61, 62 to 64, and 68 to 70 age groups, but the change had a somewhat larger effect at ages 65 to 67. Eliminating mandatory retirement altogether barely increases any of the rates up to age 67, but it has a modest effect at ages 68 to 70.

The expected net effect of most of the recent changes in policies

TABLE 7 Percentage Distribution of Work Status and Annual Hours Worked, by Age and Sex, 1977 and 1990 (High and Low Participation Series)

Hours	Ages 62 to 64			Ages 65 to 69			Ages 70 to 74			Ages 75 and Older		
	1977	1990 (Low)	1990 (High)	1977	1990 (Low)	1990 (High)	1977	1990 (Low)	1990 (High)	1977	1990 (Low)	1990 (High)
Males												
Did not work	30.1	42.9	21.8	63.2	79.1	61.2	75.8	83.6	75.7	88.0	91.0	85.0
Less than 500	4.7	3.6	4.0	6.4	6.3	6.0	4.8	4.2	4.6	2.6	—	5.4
501–1,000	8.2	11.9	9.5	8.5	4.4	8.1	5.9	5.4	6.2	3.7	—	4.3
1,001–1,500	22.3	21.0	22.6	13.4	15.2	11.5	8.3	2.8	4.3	3.7	—	2.8
1,501–2,000	19.1	11.5	17.9	6.1	3.1	8.3	4.2	1.7	3.9	1.7	—	2.8
More than 2,000	15.6	9.1	24.2	2.4	1.3	4.9	1.0	2.3	5.2	0.3	—	1.0
Mean hours worked for total population	1,083	783	1,292	407	192	484	255	166	299	144	61	122
Mean hours worked by workers	1,549	1,372	1,652	1,106	946	1,247	1,054	1,012	1,230	950	—	813
Females												
Did not work	61.3	63.5	64.1	79.6	78.5	77.8	91.6	90.1	84.9	98.6	96.8	91.3
Less than 500	5.9	5.1	3.5	4.9	7.2	4.7	2.8	4.3	3.9	—	—	3.2
501–1,000	9.8	7.6	7.4	6.3	6.2	7.1	2.8	2.2	5.4	—	—	2.7
1,001–1,500	10.1	10.3	11.5	4.3	4.7	5.8	2.0	2.4	3.5	—	—	1.8
1,501–2,000	6.6	8.5	7.9	3.6	1.8	2.4	0.3	0.8	1.4	—	—	1.0
More than 2,000	6.3	5.0	5.6	1.3	1.6	2.4	0.5	0.2	0.9	—	—	0.0
Mean hours worked for total population	481	454	474	201	181	231	68	71	135	17	21	67
Mean hours worked by workers	1,243	1,244	4,320	985	842	1,040	810	717	894	—	—	770

SOURCE: Wertheimer, R. F., and S. R. Zedlewski. 1980. *The Aging of America: A Portrait of the Elderly in 1990.* Table 18. Washington, D.C.: The Urban Institute.

TABLE 8 Total Income of Persons 65 Years of Age and Older, As a Percentage of GNP (billions of 1972 dollars)

	1980	2000	2020	2050	Rate of Growth (average annual percentage)		
					1980–2020	2020–2050	1980–2050
Total income	$100.6	$182.0	$350.2	$590.5	3.12	1.74	2.53
Income as GNP	1,423.4	1,988.4	2,526.9	3,195.2	1.43	0.78	1.16
Percentage of GNP	7.1	9.1	13.9	18.5	1.68	0.95	1.37

SOURCE: National Institute on Aging. 1984. *Macroeconomic-Demographic Model.* Table 10-34. Washington, D.C.: U.S. Government Printing Office.

on projected male labor force participation shows only modest increases in participation, which would of course reverse the trend toward earlier retirement. Similar trends are found for females as well. Of greater importance has been the total retirement income prospects of individuals, which include growing private pension support.

Projections of total income by persons over 65 years of age have been estimated by the National Institute on Aging model to the year 2050. Table 8 shows a projected increasing level of total income for older persons and an increasing proportion of this income compared with total GNP income for the country. This is particularly true up to the year 2020, with a lowered rate of growth thereafter to the middle of the next century. In terms of income per capita for older persons, there is an increasing level throughout the projection period but a progressively lower rate of increase. Judging from the previous analysis of levels of employment, it is not expected that this income will come from wages but from other sources. Nonetheless, this evidence suggests an increasingly more affluent older population and the importance of its income as a share of the income share of overall GNP. Both demographic and economic factors appear to be operating in these projections to gradually retard growth in the relative financial well-being of older persons, but the outlook is still generally favorable.

This examination of projected labor force participation and income expectations lends weight to the view that paid work among older persons is not likely to increase significantly in the future, thereby supporting the idea that other unpaid activities can be an alternative condition for sizable numbers in the growing older population. To the extent that higher proportions of women stay in the labor force until retirement, then the potential pool is diminished; but for those turning 65 the prospects are not diminished. Of course, recent changes in Social Security laws raising the entitlement age for future cohorts will have a long-term effect when and if that reform is introduced. Over the short term, however, the effect is likely to be minimal.

EDUCATION

Educational attainment has been widely viewed as a personal characteristic that is positively related to high levels of formal

TABLE 9 Educational Attainment, by Age and Sex, 1979

	Elementary		High School		College			Median Years
	1–7 Years	8 Years	Some	4 Years	Some	4 Years	5 Years+	
Male								
30–34	3.5	2.6	8.5	33.4	22.0	16.1	13.8	13.3
35–39	4.2	4.2	11.0	37.6	16.8	11.4	14.8	12.8
40–44	6.7	5.0	12.3	36.8	15.6	11.3	11.0	12.7
45–49	8.9	7.4	14.7	35.3	12.1	10.0	11.5	12.5
50–54	9.5	9.7	17.1	33.4	12.3	9.4	8.6	12.4
55–59	11.7	10.6	14.8	33.8	13.1	8.7	7.3	12.4
60–64	14.8	14.4	16.1	31.6	11.0	6.8	5.3	12.1
65–69	21.0	17.3	17.6	25.1	8.6	5.9	4.2	10.7
70–74	23.8	21.7	16.8	21.4	7.0	5.1	4.0	9.8
75+	33.3	23.9	11.3	14.6	7.5	5.5	3.7	8.7
Female								
30–34	3.3	2.4	12.1	44.5	18.4	12.1	7.3	12.7
35–39	4.1	3.1	14.7	45.9	15.8	9.0	7.2	12.6
40–44	5.5	4.5	15.7	47.3	13.3	8.5	5.0	12.5
45–49	7.2	6.0	16.7	45.5	13.3	6.5	4.8	12.4
50–54	11.7	7.4	17.2	45.5	11.9	6.3	3.6	12.4
55–59	10.0	9.4	16.2	43.4	13.0	4.9	3.2	12.3
60–64	12.5	13.4	17.8	38.8	9.1	4.3	3.4	12.2
65–69	16.3	17.4	18.5	29.9	9.0	5.6	3.2	11.5
70–74	19.3	19.7	16.8	27.2	8.6	4.8	3.3	10.7
75+	27.5	25.1	13.4	19.3	8.2	4.5	1.9	8.9

SOURCE: U.S. Bureau of the Census. 1980. "Educational Attainment in the United States: March 1979 and 1978." In *Current Population Reports*. Series P-20, No. 356, Table 2. Washington, D.C.: U.S. Government Printing Office.

participation in voluntary and service organizations. No doubt it is also important in explaining differences in self-help and activity levels generally.

There is virtual neglect in forecasting educational attainment in official population projections; the last Bureau of the Census effort at projecting education dates back to 1972. In contrast, projections of school enrollment at various levels of schooling, especially over the short term, are very common. This undoubtedly relates to the direct relevance that this information has for service and manpower planning. The 1972 projections, which were made to the year 1990, were found subsequently to be rather poor indicators of educational attainment trends for both males and females in that they overestimated the male trends and underestimated female patterns. This point is being noted because it emphasizes that projections based on previous trends or even current developments may often be distorted by cohort differences attributable to rather strong period effects. The situation in the 1960s and early 1970s was unusual in that large numbers of males remained in school to avoid the draft, thus inflating enrollments. The enrollments also were inflated by large-scale entry of veterans of military service who were entitled to educational benefits.

Instead of presenting these dated projections, a perspective on prevailing trends can be gained from the last educational attainment figures that were published from the 1979 Current Population Survey (U.S. Bureau of the Census, 1980). These figures give us a view of what future developments may be as these cohorts reach older ages. (This assumes that no differential mortality by educational status exists, no doubt a questionable assumption.)

The most noteworthy feature of Table 9 is the large increase in attainment for successively younger cohorts. Older persons at the turn of the century (beginning with the cohort aged 45 to 49) will have much higher levels of formal education and sharply lower proportions of persons who left school at the elementary or even high school level. After the turn of the century, a leveling off in median years of attainment can be anticipated for older persons and therefore a narrowing of the gap between older persons and younger cohorts. These results are in accord with recent projections of Shapiro and Easterlin (1981) on median school years completed by comparable age groups up to the year 2000.

Median education levels of males are higher than females for ages up to age 50, but a crossover takes place at that age. This does not reflect a change in college completion levels, for higher proportions of males complete college and do postgraduate work more often than females at all ages. Rather, it reflects a higher rate of completion of high school and some college for a larger share of women.

We can conclude from this rather naive approach to forecasting that the possibility of sharply increased proportions of more educated older persons could be realized by the year 2000. Thereafter, older persons on the whole will have profiles of educational attainment that are not markedly different from younger cohorts. To the extent that formal educational attainment is positively related to more productive roles, then the next few decades should witness a great improvement in this regard. Of course, at the same time we should balance this against the likelihood of higher labor force participation rates, especially for better educated women, for cohorts up to the time they reach the older ages.

HOUSEHOLDS AND MARITAL STATUS

The two characteristics households and marital status are examined together inasmuch as the types of households that are found are closely related to the marital status of persons at specified ages. The household or living arrangements in which older persons participate are clearly of major importance in determining the life conditions, social relationships, and needs that are important in assessing productive roles. The Bureau of the Census prepares projections of households based on survey information and base population projections. The latest series—up to the year 1995—was issued in 1979; therefore, it was based on the 1977 projections of population. Although somewhat outdated, they provide an indication of the likely trends that may occur in the years ahead for persons at different ages.

Nearly two-thirds of households with householders aged 55 to 64 are intact husband-wife households (Table 10). This level falls sharply with age—to about a third for families with householders 75 years of age and over. Nonfamily households, which may consist of persons living alone or with nonrelatives, are more common for females than for males, even at ages 55 to 64. The proportions in nonfamily households rise moderately with age for males but markedly for females, shifting from 16.8 percent to 45.0 per-

TABLE 10   Percentage Distribution of Households, by Types of Household and Age of Householder, 1980 and 1995 (Series C)

	1980			1995		
Type of Household	Ages 55–64	Ages 65–74	Ages 75 and Over	Ages 55–64	Ages 65–74	Ages 75 and Over
Family household						
Husband-wife	65.7	49.9	34.6	65.0	49.5	34.6
Female-no spouse	8.0	7.2	7.3	7.6	5.4	4.1
Male-no spouse	2.1	1.4	2.0	2.3	1.1	1.1
Nonfamily						
Male	7.4	8.7	11.1	9.6	10.0	9.5
Female	16.8	32.7	45.0	15.6	33.9	50.7
Total	100.0	100.0	100.0	100.0	100.0	100.0
Number (in thousands)	12,494	9,917	6,121	12,138	12,055	9,302

SOURCE: U.S. Bureau of the Census. 1979. "Projections of the Number of Households and Families: 1979 to 1995." In *Current Population Reports.* Series P-25, No. 805, Table 2. Washington, D.C.: U.S. Government Printing Office.

cent at 75 years and above. Female nonfamily households, therefore, contain many very old persons—a group generally viewed as a prime target population for special assistance. In 1980 it was estimated that there were 2.8 million such households headed by females 75 years of age and over, the vast majority of whom were living alone.

The projections reveal that little change is expected by 1995 in the proportions of family households made up of husbands and wives at the older ages. However, family households in which no spouse is present are projected to decline. Nonfamily households will increase for males under 75 but will decline for those 75 and over. Female nonfamily households will be proportionately fewer in the ages 55 to 64 but will continue to increase proportionately for women 75 years of age and older. An interesting feature brought out by the projections is the decline in the number of households expected with householders aged 55 to 64. In contrast, for older householders the increase is about 22 percent for the age category 65 to 74 and 52 percent for those 75 years and older. Once again the potential consuming population in terms of services is increasing at a more rapid pace.

These trends are largely dependent on differential patterns of

TABLE 11 Percentage Distribution of the Marital Status of the Population, by Age and Sex, 1980 and 1995 (Series C)

Marital Status	1980						1995					
	Male			Female			Male			Female		
	55–64	65–74	75+	55–64	65–74	75+	55–64	65–74	75+	55–64	65–74	75+
Single	5.6	7.5	5.6	4.6	6.7	7.1	4.7	5.9	4.9	3.2	5.4	6.2
Married, spouse present	82.2	74.2	63.2	67.2	45.8	17.3	80.2	75.2	70.2	71.7	48.8	18.3
Widowed, separated, or divorced	12.2	18.3	31.1	28.2	47.4	75.6	15.1	18.8	24.9	25.0	45.8	75.4
Number (in thousands)	10,039	6,712	3,396	11,157	8,781	6,038	9,861	7,974	4,623	10,730	10,250	8,854

SOURCE: U.S. Bureau of the Census. 1979. "Projections of the Number of Households and Families: 1979 to 1995." In *Current Population Reports*. Series P-25, No. 805, Table 4. Washington, D.C.: U.S. Government Printing Office.

mortality and survival, which have tended to keep families intact at younger ages during this period of life and produced increased widowhood at the extreme older ages. The data presented in Table 11 clearly show the impact of these factors on marital status at older ages. The proportions of both males and females who are single are small and expected to decline by 1995. Over 80 percent of males between the ages 55 to 64 are in intact marriages compared with only 67 percent for females. With increasing age the male proportion declines somewhat, but the proportion of married females with a spouse living drops sharply to a level of 17.3 percent for females 75 years of age and older. Correspondingly, the proportions of widowed, separated, and divorced (the large majority of whom are widowed at these older ages) increase moderately for males and increase greatly for females. At ages 75 and older, three-quarters of females are without a spouse.

The trend by age reflected in these projections is for males to experience intact marriages later in life. For example, a gain of 7 percentage points for males 75 and older may be noted within the category defined as married with spouse present. For females, there is a slight tendency for an increase. The proportion of widowed, separated, or divorced males is projected to increase slightly at ages up to 75, but a large decline is expected in the oldest age category. Female proportions will tend to decrease for all age groups to 1995. Although these results may seem anomalous, they are confirmed in recent cross-national research (including the United States) in which the proportions widowed appear to be declining and intact marital situations increasing, particularly for males (Myers, 1982; also see Masnick and Bane, 1980). Part of the explanation for this development lies in improved survival at younger ages for those already considered to be old, but it also reflects on the large open-ended terminal category that is often used. If more detailed older age categories are used, then the proportions of persons in intact marriages do decline for both sexes.

Longer-term projections to the year 2060 have been proposed by the Social Security Office of Actuaries for the aged population as a whole (Table 12). Some of the fluctuations in the proportions of older persons in each marital status reflect the age compositions of the aged population. This is true for married and widowed categories, in particular, in which there are declines, then

TABLE **12**   Marital Status of Population 65 Years and Over in the Social Security Area, by Sex, United States, 1980–2060

Year	Total	Single	Married	Widowed	Divorced
			NUMBER		
Male					
1980	10,397	600	7,686	1,688	424
2000	14,232	716	10,128	2,118	1,270
2020	21,567	1,236	15,730	2,743	1,858
2040	26,841	1,951	18,798	3,794	2,299
2060	28,160	2,196	19,848	3,602	2,514
Female					
1980	15,544	940	5,989	8,024	590
2000	21,767	980	8,092	9,962	2,734
2020	30,904	1,597	12,606	11,513	5,188
2040	39,788	2,289	15,473	16,184	5,842
2060	41,618	2,548	16,185	16,693	6,192
Total					
1980	25,941	1,540	13,675	9,712	1,014
2000	35,999	1,696	18,220	12,080	4,004
2020	52,471	2,833	28,336	14,256	7,046
2040	66,629	4,240	34,271	19,978	8,141
2060	69,778	4,744	36,033	20,295	8,706
			PERCENTAGE		
Male					
1980	100.0	5.8	73.9	16.2	4.1
2000	100.0	5.0	71.2	14.9	8.9
2020	100.0	5.7	72.9	12.7	8.6
2040	100.0	7.3	70.0	14.1	8.6
2060	100.0	7.8	70.5	12.8	8.9
Female					
1980	100.0	6.0	38.5	51.6	3.8
2000	100.0	4.5	37.2	45.8	12.6
2020	100.0	5.2	40.8	37.2	16.8
2040	100.0	5.8	38.9	40.7	14.7
2060	100.0	6.14	38.9	40.1	14.9
Total					
1980	100.0	5.9	52.7	37.4	3.9
2000	100.0	4.7	50.6	33.6	11.1
2020	100.0	5.4	54.0	27.2	13.4
2040	100.0	6.4	51.4	30.0	12.2
2060	100.0	6.8	51.6	29.1	12.5

SOURCE: U.S. Department of Health and Human Services. 1980. *United States Population Projection by Marital Status for OASDI Cost Estimates, 1980.* Actuarial Study No. 84. Washington, D.C.: U.S. Government Printing Office.

increases, then declines. The general pattern, however, is toward lower proportions of widowed persons, especially females; some increase in single persons; and large gains in the proportions of both male and female divorced persons. While these percentage figures do not reveal any major changes in the marital categories (e.g., single, widowed, divorced) that might be expected to lead toward greater dependence, it should be kept in mind that large numerical gains are characteristics of all of the categories as the overall aged population increases. In terms of service requirements, it is the number of persons requiring assistance that is of paramount importance.

These findings about trends in household patterns, particularly for females living alone and in nonfamilial circumstances, suggest that the demand for services may well increase, especially at the oldest ages, but that persons in intact marriages may be both relatively and numerically more numerous and, therefore, be in positions for supplying services.

KINSHIP RELATIONS

The extent to which unpaid productive roles relate to mutual aid for other family members must necessarily be influenced by the potential kinship networks that exist. Demographic trends pointing to steadily declining mortality at older ages, which increases survival, and continued low fertility levels have modified family structures by altering the number of siblings, children, and multigenerational families. Of particular importance for the topic is the increased likelihood that persons entering the older age categories will themselves have parents still living. Ceteris paribus, this creates new and rather different needs for mutual aid to parents, at the same time limiting the pool of persons available to provide aid to other nonfamily individuals or organizations.

Several modeling approaches may be taken to derive estimates of available kin, and various analyses already have been made to capture those dynamics (Hammel et al., 1981; Pullum, 1982). Wolf (1983) has made the most recent effort to model the process, and some results from his projection study are presented in Table 13. The data are presented only for males inasmuch as the results for females are quite similar.

The probability of a male being 65 to 69 years of age and

TABLE 13 Probability of Different Kinship Relations for Males in Forecast Year, by Birth Cohort

	Retirement History Survey							
Year of Birth =	1906–1910	1921–1925	1926–1930	1931–1935	1936–1940	1941–1945	1946–1950
Forecast Year =	1975	1990	1995	2000	2005	2010	2015
Available kin variables:[a]							
Father alive	.014	.026	.034	.039	.048	.054	.060
Mother alive	.060	.140	.174	.196	.225	.234	.243
Any living parents	.072	.159	.197	.222	.257	.269	.281
Any living children	.833	.891	.393	.912	.908	.884	.845

[a]These figures are probabilities.

SOURCE: From Douglas A. Wolf. 1983. *Kinship and the Living Arrangements of Older Americans.* Washington, D.C.: The Urban Institute.

having a father still alive was .014 in 1975; it increases to .06 by the year 2015. The probability of having a mother alive at these ages is much higher, as expected, and it increases in 2015 to a level in which a quarter of the males would be in this situation. The probabilities of having any living parent alive is naturally higher. Having at least one sibling alive is more sensitive to prior fertility (note the dip in 1921–1925 and later cohorts), but the levels are very high, reaching 88 percent in 2015. Finally, having a living child rises to 91 percent in the year 2000 for males aged 65 to 69 but then declines gradually to 84 percent in 2015. This reflects the present "birth dearth," and assumes low fertility levels for the near future.

It is likely, then, that there will be an enlarged pool of family members for whom mutual aid may be necessary. In turn, younger family members (at ages 65 to 69) are also available who could provide assistance if someone was in need. The term "potential" must be emphasized, inasmuch as the family support system depends on many other factors as well. These figures suggest that mortality conditions play a somewhat greater role than fertility in the structure of family relations and touch upon a whole range of issues relating to living arrangements, migratory patterns, and mutual aid and assistance.

HEALTH STATUS

There have been relatively few attempts to forecast the health status of the older population. One recent effort by the National Center for Health Statistics uses fairly conventional procedures of ratio estimation for different health dimensions applied to projections by age and sex. As will be noted subsequently, alternative conceptualizations of the issue are also possible. Table 14 provides the main conclusions from this study using two different mortality assumptions in the projections for contrast.

Even if we consider the projections under the unrealistic assumption of constant mortality, by the year 2003 the impact of the aging population may be clearly noted on all of the health dimensions examined. Declining mortality shows large increases over the 25-year period in terms of persons with limitations of activity, hospital short-stay visits, and especially nursing home residency (the number of such residents more than doubles under the assumed ratios). Physician visits are the least likely to

TABLE 14 Health Statistics for Persons 65 Years of Age and Older, 1978 and 2003

	Total for All Ages			Total for 65+			Percentage: 65+ of Total		
	1978	Constant Mortality, 2003	Declining Mortality, 2003	1978	Constant Mortality, 2003	Declining Mortality, 2003	1978	Constant Mortality, 2003	Declining Mortality, 2003
HEALTH CONDITIONS									
Persons with limitation of activity due to chronic conditions (in thousands)	31,212	42,492	45,811	10,893	15,000	17,866	34.9	35.3	39.0
Physician visits (in millions)	1,072	1,357.8	1,410.6	164	220	259.6	15.3	16.2	18.4
Days of care in short-stay hospitals (in millions)	274.1	372.0	406.8	100.3	142.5	173.7	36.6	38.3	42.7
Nursing home residents (in millions)	1,322.2	2,072.6	2,804.4	1,147.7	1,857	2,585.6	86.8	89.6	92.2
HEALTH EXPENDITURES (in billions of dollars)									
Physician services	36.3	47.2	49.6	8.1	10.9	12.8	22.3	23.1	25.8
Hospital care	73.9	97.5	105.8	20.5	29.0	35.5	27.7	29.8	33.6
Nursing home care	14.5	22.6	30.3	12.1	19.6	27.3	83.4	86.7	90.1

SOURCE: National Center for Health Statistics. 1983. "Changing Mortality Patterns, Health Services Utilization and Health Care Expenditures: United States, 1978–2003." In *Analytical and Epidemiological Studies.* Series 3, No. 23. Washington, D.C.: U.S. Government Printing Office.

increase markedly. Nonetheless, the relative burden of health care requirements for the older population would appear to be a major cause of concern for the health care system. Many of these dimensions also would lead to increased demand for informal care—for example, for the nearly 40 percent of the population with limitations of activity represented by aged persons.

In terms of health expenditures these projections show the growth in fiscal liability generated by the aging population. For these three services the 1978 expenditures of $124.7 billion increase to $167.3 and $185.7 billion in the year 2003 under the two mortality assumptions. The aged share of these expenditures increases from 32.6 percent to 35.6 and 40.7 percent, respectively, in 2003. The cost gains are particularly large in terms of nursing home care, exceeding even the aged expenditure increases for hospital care. Thus, both the demand for services and expenditures are highly sensitive to demographic changes generated by an aging population. Figures such as these, which are undoubtedly underestimates, are the impetus for increased calls for attention to alternative types of community and family care that might complement the formal health care system.

Consideration of health status is quite different from the other characteristics discussed earlier in that the outcome variable is itself part of the input to a projective model. It has been argued that appropriate demographic projections will have to relate changes in the age structure of the over-65 population (which are, to a large part, a function of mortality at those ages) to the associated morbidity and disability changes. Thus, such projections must forecast mortality, morbidity, and disability (loss of functional capacity) as correlated phenomena, each driven by the underlying processes of physiological aging.

Perhaps the simplest way to appreciate the age implications of the biomedical correlation of mortality, morbidity, and disability is to consider Figure 1. In this figure, the horizontal axis represents age and the vertical axis represents the proportion of a birth cohort that would survive to a given age without experiencing a particular type of health status change. The three curves in the figure represent the trajectory of change in the age-specific probability of the event. Specifically, the first curve (A) represents the simple probability of survival to age x. A second curve (B) represents the probability that a person will survive to age x without suffering serious limitations of activity. Curve (C) indi-

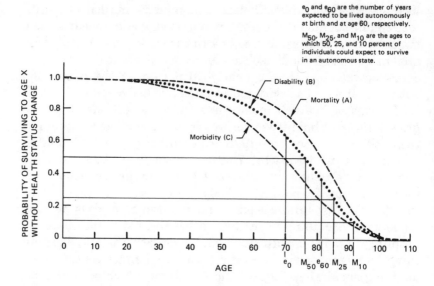

FIGURE 1   Mortality, morbidity, and disability survival curves.

cates survival without a morbid condition. The figure thus clearly represents (1) the changing age correlation of mortality and disability and (2) the age dynamics that cause the prevalence of disease and disability to rise in conjunction with a rise in the risk of mortality. The figure also defines the question: Given changes in survival (A), how does the prevalence of disease and disability in the population change? Clearly, this latter question is of critical importance in determining both the demand for various types of volunteer services among the elderly and the potential pool of elderly who are healthy and able to provide such services.

Although the need for projections giving the age change in the relation of mortality to other health status is clear, such projections rarely have been performed. This is rather surprising because the data requirements for such projections are not as great as they first appear. One example is provided in a simulation study of population aging in Japanese society conducted by Nihon University (1982). In an analysis by Koizumi (1982), data from standard vital statistics life tables were combined with information from three nationally representative surveys of health characteristics, health service utilization, and welfare.

The results from such analyses were used to interrelate morbidity, health status changes, perception of subjective health status, health service utilization, and mortality over age. As such they are relevant to both supply and demand issues.

These relations can be examined in an example using U.S. data, which is presented in Figure 2. In this figure, data on heart and hypertensive disease and limitations are combined with the survival probabilities derived from a standard U.S. life table. As we can see, the age-specific prevalence of morbidity rises initially and is followed secondarily by a rapid increase in disability at later ages.

The use of projections that interrelate various population health states in this way does not resolve all of the issues in assessing health, health service utilization, and the implications of health for the supply of and demand for volunteer services. However, it does provide information on the basic parameters of such behavior for the system. The fact that relatively little effort has been applied to resolving the nature of such associations on a population level—let alone forecasting such relations into the future—indicates some serious gaps in the information base needed to plan for the requirements of an aging U.S. population.

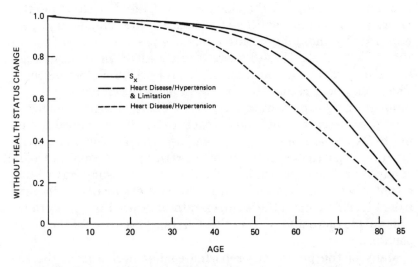

FIGURE 2 Survival curves for the 1978 U.S. population and for heart disease and hypertension, with and without limitation.

DISCUSSION

Clearly, population projections are needed in order to create an awareness of the social changes that are occurring in a society and that are likely to occur in the future. Although demographers and other statistical scientists began to make such projections in the nineteenth century, it is only in the past 50 years that systematic and periodic projections have become commonplace. For example, the first systematic projections of the U.S. population were made in 1934 by the U.S. National Resources Board and prepared by Thompson and Whelpton. And it was not until 1947 that the Bureau of the Census began to prepare projections as a regular activity. In this half century there has been a growing acknowledgment that population projections are an integral part of the planning process for government agencies on all levels and for business enterprises and the like. With this increased demand has emerged a continuing need for more disaggregated projections that relate more proximally to the specific components of the population of interest, that is, the conditions of the aged population itself.

The projections from which data have been drawn for this review are basically general projections of the total population that have been made with little specific attention to particular dynamics of change at the older stages of life. For example, the issues raised about health status indicate the complex and perhaps rapidly changing nature of disease prevalence and disability at older ages. These factors directly affect mortality rates, which play such an important role in projections of older persons. The rather poor record that has been achieved in projecting the numbers of aged persons in the past reflects on the inadequacy of mortality forecasts that failed to capture the dramatic declines in mortality at older ages during the past decade. The changes in labor force participation at points of retirement demand careful single-year-of-age determinations, but these issues have only recently been pursued and no current data are available in published form. In short there appears to be a need for projections that devote more attention to the dynamic properties of the older population.

Many of the projections reported earlier derive from the so-called official projections of the U.S. Bureau of the Census in the sense that they apply ratios of the subject matter to the projected age-sex-race base population figures (Long, 1981). This is true of projections of educational attainment, households, marital status, labor force, and the like. In spite of the apparent linkage between these projections, the different efforts that go into them are generally uncoordinated. We find the projections beginning at different years and being carried forward for different time periods, the use of varying age categories, and release at different points in time. This may be disconcerting to the users, but it also reflects on the lack of systematic interplay of crucial dimensions within the projections themselves. For example, labor force projections are made without consideration of such factors as educational attainment and marital status. Mortality or fertility trends are developed without consideration of labor force or marital status. The components, therefore, are not interrelated on the conceptual level, and this is carried through to the technical level.

It is not surprising, then, that organizations outside the federal government have developed their own projection models. The microsimulation model DYNASIM created by the Urban Institute, the macroeconomic-demographic model used by ICF Incorporated, and the macro model used by the Joint Center for Urban Studies of MIT and Harvard University are cases in point. But although studies using these more sophisticated models are often of great interest, there is an even greater diversity in the modes of presenting results from these studies than there is in the federally produced series. This circumstance makes reviewing the findings difficult and interpreting discrepancies virtually impossible.

To summarize, this brief review has pointed to a number of conceptual, technical, and organizational factors that limit the use of current projections for planning and policy formulation purposes. While we are not suggesting that a single set of projections should be developed and strictly adhered to in the federal government, we do think that greater coordination would be desirable. There also is a clear need to examine more sophisticated models of both inputs in projections (i.e., mortality, fertility, migration) as well as outcomes (e.g., educational attainment, health status). This may be accomplished by using more structurally dynamic analytic models, such as multistate mathematical applications that include increment-decrement life table approaches, and biomedical models of the sickness-death process.

Moreover, adequate assessment of the accuracy of population projections should be an ongoing activity. Current development suggests that the time may be appropriate for providing information about confidence limits at the time projections are issued (Keyfitz, 1981, 1982; Stoto, 1983). In short, we are suggesting that projections be given a higher research priority than has previously been the case. The National Academy of Sciences could well play an important role as a catalyst in this development.

REFERENCES

Anderson, J. M., and W. McNaught. 1982. *Projecting Alternative Futures for the Retirement Income System.* Final report to the National Institute on Aging. Washington, D.C.: ICF, Inc.

Ascher, W. 1978. *Forecasting: An Appraisal for Policymakers and Planners.* Baltimore, Md.: Johns Hopkins University Press.

Hammel, E. A., K. W. Wachter, and C. K. McDaniel. 1981. "The Kin of the Aged in A.D. 2000: The Chickens Come Home to Roost." PP. 11–39 in S. B. Kiesler, N. Morgan, and V. K. Oppenheimer, eds. *Aging: Social Change.* New York: Academic Press.

Hendricks, G., and J. R. Storey. 1981. *The Long-Run Effects of Alternative Mandatory Retirement Policies.* Washington, D.C.: The Urban Institute.

Keyfitz, N. 1981. "The Limits of Population Forecasting." *Population and Development Review* 8(4):579–593.

Keyfitz, N. 1982. "Can Knowledge Improve Forecasts?" *Population and Development Review* 8 (4):729–751.

Koizumi, A. 1982. "Toward a Healthy Life in the 21st Century." Chapter 6 (pp. 6–1 and 6–19) in *Population Aging in Japan: Problems and Policy Issues in the 21st Century.* International Symposium on an Aging Society: Strategies for 21st Century Japan, November 24–27, Nihon University.

Long, J.F. 1981. "Survey of Federally Produced National Level Demographic Projections," *Review of Public Data Use* 9:309–329.

Masnick, G., and M. J. Bane. 1980. *The Nations Families: 1960–1990.* An Outlook Report of the Joint Center for Urban Studies of MIT and Harvard University.

Myers, G. C. 1982. "Cross-national Variations in Marital Status Among The Elderly." Paper presented at Gerontological Society of America Meetings, Boston, Massachusetts.

National Center for Health Statistics. 1983. "Changing Mortality Patterns, Health Services Utilization and Health Care Expenditures: United States, 1978–2003." In *Analytical and Epidemiological Studies.* Series 3, No. 23. Washington, D.C.: U.S. Government Printing Office.

National Institute on Aging. 1982. *A National Plan for Research on Aging: Report of the National Research on Aging Planning Panel.* Washington, D.C.: U.S. Government Printing Office.

National Institute on Aging. 1984. *Macroeconomic-Demographic Model.* Washington, D.C.: U.S. Government Printing Office.

Nihon University. 1982. "Population-Aging in Japan: Problems and Policy Issues in the 21st Century." Paper presented at the International Symposium on an Aging Society: Strategies for 21st Century Japan, November 24–27.

Pullum, T. W. 1982. "The Eventual Frequencies of Kin in a Stable Population." *Demography* 19:549–565.

Rosow, I. 1976. "Status and Role Change Through the Life Span." In R. H. Binstock and E. Shanas, eds. *Handbook of Aging and the Social Sciences.* New York: Van Nostrand Reinhold.

Shapiro, M. O., and R. A. Easterlin. 1981. "Educational Attainment by Sex and Age, 1980–2000." *Review of Public Data Use* (9):323–329.

Stoto, M. A. 1983. "The Accuracy of Population Projections." *Journal of the American Statistical Association* (18):13–20.

U.S. Bureau of Labor Statistics. 1982. *Economic Projections to 1990.* Bulletin 2121. Washington, D.C.: U.S. Government Printing Office.

U.S. Bureau of Labor Statistics. 1984. *Employment Projections for 1995.* Bulletin 2197, Appendix A-1. Washington, D.C.: U.S. Government Printing Office.

U.S. Bureau of the Census. 1979. "Projections of the Number of Households and Families: 1979 to 1995." In *Current Population Reports.* Series P-25, No. 805. Washington, D.C.: U.S. Government Printing Office.

U.S. Bureau of the Census. 1980. "Educational Attainment in the United States: March 1979 and 1978." In *Current Population Reports.* Series P-20, No. 356. Washington, D.C.: U.S. Government Printing Office.

U.S. Bureau of the Census. 1983. "Provisional Projections of the Population of the United States by Age and Sex: 1980 to 2000." In *Current Population Reports.* Series P-25, No. 917. Washington, D.C.: U.S. Government Printing Office.

U.S. Bureau of the Census. 1984. "Projections of the Population of the United States, by Age, Sex, and Race: 1983 to 2080." In *Current Population Reports.* Series P-25, No. 952. Washington, D.C.: U.S. Government Printing Office.

U.S. Department of Health and Human Services, Social Security Administration, Office of the Actuary. 1980. *United States Population Projection by Marital Status for OASDI Cost Estimates, 1980.* Actuarial Study No. 84. Washington, D.C.: U.S. Government Printing Office.

Wertheimer, R. F., and S. R. Zedlewski. 1980. *The Aging of America: A Portrait of the Elderly in 1990.* Washington, D.C.: The Urban Institute.

Wolf, D. A. 1983. *Kinship and the Living Arrangements of Older Americans.* Washington, D.C.: The Urban Institute.

Index